Ambrose Macaulay

3 June 1974.

HUMANISM AND CHRISTIANITY

PERSPECTIVES
IN HUMANISM
Planned and Edited by
RUTH NANDA ANSHEN

Board of Editors

HUMANISM
AND
CHRISTIANITY

MARTIN C.
D'ARCY

CONSTABLE
LONDON

IMPRIMATUR
De licentia Superiorum Ordinis

Published by Constable and Company Ltd
10 Orange Street, London W.C.2
First published by The New American Library, Inc.
in association with The World Publishing Company
2231 West 110th Street, Cleveland, Ohio 44102

Copyright © 1969 and 1971 by Martin C. D'Arcy

'Perspectives in Humanism: The Future of Tradition'
Copyright © 1967 and 1969 by Ruth Nanda Anshen

ISBN 0 09 458150 9

Reproduced and Printed in Great Britain by
Redwood Press Limited, Trowbridge & London

CONTENTS

ACKNOWLEDGEMENTS

Humanism and Christianity was first published in the 'Perspectives in Humanism' Series by World Publishing Company, New York, in 1969. This series was edited by Ruth Nanda Anshen, whose introductory essay, 'The Future of Tradition', is reprinted here by contractual obligation.

The author and publisher gratefully acknowledge permission to quote verse from the following works:

W. H. Auden: *Collected Shorter Poems* (Faber & Faber).
Roy Campbell: *The Collected Poems* (The Bodley Head).
David Jones: *Anathemata, Epoch and Artist, In Parenthesis,* and *The Hunt* (Faber & Faber).
Dr. Kathleen W. Hughes: *The Church in Early Anglo-Irish Society* (Methuen).

PERSPECTIVES IN HUMANISM
THE FUTURE OF TRADITION
RUTH NANDA ANSHEN

Perspectives in Humanism is designed to affirm that the world, the universe, and man are remarkably stable, elementally unchanging. Protons remain protons, and the other known elements are themselves, even when their atoms are broken; and man remains, in his essence, man. Every form of nature possesses what Aristotle called its own law. The blade of grass does not exist to feed the cow; the cow does not exist in order to give milk to man; and man does not exist to be subdivided, for to subdivide him is to execute him. Man is an organism, a whole, in which segregation of any sort is artificial and in which every phenomenon is a manifestation of the whole. The lawfulness of nature, including man's nature, is a miracle defying understanding.

My Introduction to this Series is not of course to be construed as a prefatory essay for each individual book. These few pages simply attempt to set forth the general aim and purpose of the Series as a whole. They try to point to the humanistic significance of the respective disciplines as represented by those scholars who have been invited to participate in this endeavor.

Perspectives in Humanism submits that there is a constant process of continuity within the process of change. This process lies in the very nature of man. We ask ourselves: What is this constant? What is it that endures and is the foundation of our intellectual and moral civilization? What is it that we are able to call our humanistic tradition? What is it that must survive and be transmitted to the future if man is to remain human?

The answer is that this constant lies in recognizing what is changeless in the midst of change. It is that heritage of timeless and immutable values on which we can fix our gaze whenever the language of change and decline which history speaks seems to become too overwhelming for the human heart. It offers us the spectacle of the constancy of certain basic forms and ideas throughout a process of continuous social mutations, intellectual development, and scientific revolution. The constant is the original form maintaining itself by transformation and adapting itself to changing social conditions, the continuity which is the very medium of change.

It is the loss of awareness of this constant in our time, not through the failure but rather through the very success of our modern scientific and technological achievements that has produced a society in which it becomes increasingly difficult to live a life that is human.

Perspectives in Humanism tries to confront, and, if possible, show the way to the resolution of, the major dilemma of our epoch: the greatest affliction of the modern mind. This dilemma is created by the magnificent fruits of the industrial revolution on the one hand and by an inexorable technology on the other. It is the acceptance of power as a source of authority and as a substitute for truth and knowledge. It is the dilemma born out of a skepticism in values and a faith in the perfectibility of the mind. It accepts the results of scientific inquiry as carrying self-evident implications, an obvious error. And finally it defines knowledge as a product, accepting lines of force emptied of lines of will, rather than, as indeed it is, a process.

The authors in this Series attempt to show the failure of what has been called scientific humanism, to show the limitation of scientific method which determines only sequences of events without meaning and among these events none more meaningless than man. For modern science is not concerned with human experience, nor with human purposes, and its knowledge of ascertained natural facts can never represent the whole of human nature. Now man is crying out for the recognition of insights derived from other sources, from the awareness that the problem of mechanism and teleology is a legitimate problem, requiring a humanistic solution.

It has always been on the basis of the hypothesis that the world and man's place in it can be understood by reason that the world and man become intelligible. And in all the crises of the mind and heart it has been the belief in the possibility of a solution that has made a solution possible.

Studies of man are made in all institutions of research and higher learning. There is hardly a section of the total scholarly enterprise which does not contribute directly or indirectly to our knowledge of man's nature. Not only philosophy and theology, not only history and the other humanities, not only psychology, sociology, biology, and medicine investigate man's nature and existence, but also the natural sciences do so, at least indirectly, and even directly, whenever they reflect upon their own methods, limits, and purposes.

It is in the light of such considerations that *Perspectives in Humanism* endeavors to show the false antinomy between the scientist and the humanist and the Cartesian error of dualizing mind and body. This Series tries to point to the incoherence of our time which implies the breakdown of integrative relationships, and to demonstrate that in science, as in all other fields of human thought and action, humanism may be preserved only through channels of shared experience and through mutual hopes. Indeed, humanism in these volumes is defined as that force which may render science once more part of universal human discourse. In this, it is here proposed, lies the future of tradition. Our search is for the "ought" which does not derive from facts alone.

In many realms of scholarly work there is an awareness of the fragmentation of man. And there is an increasing recognition that the study of man-made and natural ecological systems is as necessary as the study of isolated particles and elementary reactions. Most impressive has been the reaction of many scientists to the problems of the "atomic age" created by the technical application of their own theories. They realize that the question of the human meaning of scientific research cannot be repressed any longer in view of the immensity of these problems.

In biology and medicine the qualitative uniqueness of every life process, and especially the uniqueness of that process which is called human, has come into the foreground of investigation. And, above all, biology, psychology, and medicine have made parallel efforts to overcome the accepted but untenable split between the psychological and the physiological aspects of human nature, remembering with Aristotle that the soul is the meaning of the body.

Historical studies in all directions, including political, social, economic, cultural, and religious history, have begun to ask the question: What are the characteristics of man as they are manifested in history? The exclusively factual and causal approach to history generally, and its special divisions such as history of the arts, of literature, of societal forms, of religion, has been broken down in many places. The question of meaning has not replaced the question of fact but has given research another dimension and a direct relevance for man's self-interpretation.

This is the situation. No convincing picture of man has arisen in spite of the many ways in which human thought has tried to reach it. But one thing has been achieved: The problem has made itself felt with great force in many places in spite of considerable resistance. This alone would justify a concentrated attempt to seek for preliminary answers and new questions resulting from them. And this is the aim of *Perspectives in Humanism*.

There is, however, another rather serious reason for cooperation in the study of this new and enlarged meaning of humanism. It is the fact that, under the impact of these developments, a linguistic confusion in all important matters of man's existence has taken place in the Western world—a confusion which makes cooperation extremely difficult. Most concepts used in scholarly attempts to draw a picture of man are ambiguous, or obsolete, or fashionable clichés. It is impossible *not* to use them, but they mislead if they are used. This is not a recent development—although the methods of contemporary publicity have supported it and are one of the greatest impediments to healing it—but it is a result of the intellectual and social history of the last centuries. A change is possible only if this history in all its ramifications is studied from the point of view of the disintegration of the language concerning man which has taken place in the last centuries. Such a dialogue is formidable and must be done in terms of a continuous exchange between representatives of the different spheres of knowledge and of cultures. It is our hope that this Series will provide favorable conditions for such an exchange.

The historical approach must be done in interdependence with a systematic approach. Concepts developed in one sphere must show their relevance for other spheres. This also is being done in a casual way in contemporary literature. It must be done methodologically. The departmental boundaries must be trespassed continuously. It is ultimately impossible to make a true statement about the physiological dynamics of the human body without taking into consideration the spirit which forms the flesh. It is ultimately impossible to describe the self-destructive tendencies in a neurotic person without describing the structures of estrangement in man's social existence. These examples can be increased indefinitely. They show that the departmentalization of our knowledge of man, although it was and is a matter of expediency, is at the same time a cause for distortion. Here lies the main positive task of *Perspectives in Humanism*.

Humanism is the ideal pattern supposed to reveal the true nature of man and the task for which he was born—the task of shaping himself into a true man and thereby creating a society worthy of him to be transmitted to future generations. For humanism is a lasting truth, not merely a transitory historical phenomenon. Like the changeless *logos* of which Heraclitus spoke, it pervades the whole process of eternal flux, and may even be said to be like a divine fire that works in each of us whether we know it or not. There stands behind our Western tradition, just as behind the great traditions of the East, a common metaphysical faith which transcends all schisms and conflicts within it.

And just as humanism means that there exists a common humanity beyond all divisiveness, so humanism also means that a unitary nature unites scientist and humanist alike. It can no longer be said that man is either a scientist or a humanist. The knower and the known, the doubter and the doubt, are one. To identify the scientist with a single method, the scientific one, that is, with a single procedure, is a distortion of science. All the powers of the mind, of intuition, of observation (to which the observer brings his own perception), of discursive and nondiscursive knowledge, are brought into play in the achievement of scientific interpretation. And the preanalytic data of science, if called "facts," are in reality but problematic facts. The only facts initially given for exploration are the facts of humanistic relevance, facts laden or saturated with loose or crude interpretations and demanding therefore reinterpretations by procedures free from what Bacon described as idols of the mind.

The difference between humanistic and scientific meaning is a difference not of kind but of degree. Can it be seriously maintained that, prior to the advent of scientific knowledge, with its elaborate hypotheses and theories, all intent upon the search for the nature of things, men were acquainted merely with sense data, or meaningless impressions? Prescientific knowledge is also knowledge, involving in incipient or inchoate form most of the activities in which science is engaged, such as naming and classifying, numbering and measuring, describing and explaining. And all these aspects are but the humanistic yearning in man's nature to establish a legitimate place for himself in the cosmic scheme from which he feels that he has been estranged. However farflung its hypotheses or comprehensive its theories, science has no objects for its application save such as can be known through a humanistic interpretation and therefore known through perception suffused with judgment and belief. Science plunges into the phenomena, isolated and apart from the wholeness of reality, interpreting with precision and even accuracy and by devices that make possible more adequate inferences, and sometimes even more reliable predictions, the very same world of things which are antecedently recognized through the implicit perceptions of humanistic insights.

What this Series hopes to demonstrate is that humanism by its nature is intent upon forcing the mind to make, since it is unable not to make, judgments of value. It is to accept once more the validity of the metaphysical hypothesis. What humanism desires and demands is an insight into the meaning of the universe of nature and of man as totality by the use of categories more general or pervasive than those required for the things segmented by a special science. The antihumanist prejudice, prevalent in certain quarters, can be explained only by the dogma that the universe and man in it are everlastingly divided among and by the special sciences, the synopsis of each being separate and exclusive so that a categorial synopsis of the total nature of the thing remains *a priori* precluded.

It is the endeavor of *Perspectives in Humanism* to show that there is no knowledge (knowledge which is synonymous with being) save by a humanistic perception of what we know. For we bring ourselves to every objective act of cognition, we are always intimately involved in every cognitive act. And we can no longer allow ourselves to separate thought from feeling nor to push our subjective experiences into the cognitively irrelevant corner of the emotions (of which poetry, religion, metaphysics, and morality are supposed to be expressions). Knowledge which is at the same time humanistic will then be seen to have a no less legitimate claim than that of any science.

In other words this Series attempts to affirm the truth that man's knowledge can be made relevant to life only by including a knowledge about knowledge. And therefore the humanist can no longer be isolated from the scientist nor can he defend, as he did in the Renaissance, his own studies against the claims of other disciplines. For the humanist even as the scientist has to face the problem of truth, a problem which may be treated in multiple ways, retaining the emphasis, however, on the quest for unity, for that which is constant, in the face of apparently divergent and incompatible doctrines. *Perspectives in Humanism* suggests that one of man's fundamental concerns, be he scientist, philosopher, theologian, artist, or political thinker, is the humanist authority which derives from truth and not the technological authority which derives from power.

Humanism, it is shown here, differs from the specific humanisms of past history in that it forces the mind again and again to recognize wider and subtler relations, lifting seemingly unrelated patterns into a higher harmony. A knowledge of past humanisms is of course indispensable, since some of this knowledge is intrinsically valid and true, and we are summoned to recognize this before we can make significant contributions to our own humanism. This is the heritage each generation is called upon to transmit to the future. It is the humanist heritage which is synonymous with a doctrine of man, explored, enriched, and enlarged for the benefit of mankind and society.

Humanism as presented in this Series affirms the dependence of cultural values on concrete realities. We cannot conceive the former apart from the latter any more than we can conceive a painting apart from its pigment and canvas. And the unity, the constant, in both instances belongs to the realm of values. Therein lie their essence, meaning, and reality. And it is no difficult task to show that those who reject such interpretations in the name of scientific method, of blood, of property, or of economic necessity, and are therefore scornful of humanism as an ineffective phantasm, are themselves actuated to this scorn by dogmas, ideologies, or other value-impregnated thought forms, which can come to terms with the former only in the eternal arena of humanistic ideas.

The socialist program of humanism as envisaged by the communists has failed, and henceforth we cannot speak of the problem of Man as having significance only after the collapse of capitalism. For to offer man only what is human is to betray him and to wish him ill, since by the principal part of him which is the mind and the heart man is called to something better than a merely historical or physical life. As Aristotle reminds us, "To propose to man a merely human end is to misunderstand nature."

It is clear that whoever uses the term humanism (and the term itself is ambiguous) brings into play at once an entire metaphysic, and the idea we form of humanism will have wholly different implications according to whether we hold or do not hold that there is in the nature of man a constant, an essence, something which breathes an air outside of time and a personality whose profoundest needs transcend time and space, and even the self.

The authors in this Series try to show that humanism is the essence of all disciplines of the human mind. Humanism indeed tends to render man more truly human. It makes man's original greatness manifest itself by causing him to participate in all that can enrich him in nature and in history by concentrating the universe in man and by dilating man to the universe. This Series endeavors to show how, through humanism, man may make use of all the potentialities he holds within him, his creative powers and the life of reason, and how he may make the powers of the physical world the instruments of his freedom.

The question raised by the authors here is: Can humanism become aware of itself and significant to man only in those moments of despair, at a time of the dissipation of its own energies, of isolation, alienation, loss of identity, dissociation, and descent; only when pain opens man's eyes and he sees and finds his burden unendurable? Does this lead to the proliferation of that atomic anarchy of which Nietzsche has spoken and which Dostoevsky's Grand Inquisitor offers us as a picture of a threatening fate, the nihilism of our time? Is there a humanism conscious of itself and free, leading man to sacrifice and greatness, which is indeed transcendent because here human suffering and consciousness of responsibility open man's eyes? For it is on the humanist answer to this question (and the grounds on which it is decided) that the various positions men take in the face of the travail of history enacted before our eyes and the diverse practical decisions which they feel obliged to make, do in fact depend.

Perspectives in Humanism tries to work toward defining a sound and sane philosophy of modern history so desperately needed. The authors in this Series work to substitute for the inhuman system currently confronting us a new form of civilization which would outline and represent humanism both sacred and secular. *Perspectives in Humanism* tries to show that this humanism is all the more human since it does not worship man but has a real and effective respect for human dignity and for the rights of human personality.

Our age, like every other, is in the grip of its own changing and conflicting thought forms, but the scholar who deals with "facts" cannot achieve objectivity by denuding these "facts" of value, for if he treats them as nonvalues he does not treat them at all. The best he can aspire to is the catholic comprehension and the tolerance that find nothing alien in anything human. Humanism requires that we interpret in our own terms, in the terms of our culture, the total given reality, persistently evaluating it all, means and ends in one, together with the sustaining earth and the indifferent cosmos, and thereby transmuting fact not only into value but also into symbol. This is its necessity, its life, as well as its peril.

The Chinese ideograph, the symbol of humanism, on the jacket and binding of each volume in this Series is found on early Chinese bronzes in the year 1200 B.C. It reflects the vision and image not of an individual man but all of mankind. It is the symbol chosen for the ability of man to transcend his own isolated self, a quality fundamental to his humanity. The "objectivity" of science cannot help man in his present human predicament, since for science in this sense there can be no commitment. So that in the end we know everything but understand nothing. In fact, we would seek nothing, not being motivated by concern for any question. It is a symbol which is concise, not precise; it is reflective, not descriptive. It is the impersonal self, identical from man to man, and is even perhaps similar to the essence of all life in its manifold expressions in nature. This symbol * thereby shows us why, in our search for meaning, direction, historical unities, and experience in science or in life, we must give logical priority as well as metaphysical preeminence to what we call, for lack of a better term, humanism: that which has something in common with intellectual achievement, with moral action, and with love.

* I am indebted and grateful to Professor Chiang Yee, Professor of Art and Calligraphy at Columbia University. He has generously drawn my attention to this ideograph.

R.N.A.

HUMANISM
AND
CHRISTIANITY

MARTIN C.
D'ARCY

CHAPTER 1
MODERN HUMANISM

Preestablished absurdity is now the option in place of preestablished harmony.

"Don't take on, dearie. Be a philosopher and don't think about it."
(Heard on a London bus)

An epoch of mindless Abelards and Galileos who are having the time of their lives.

In every generation there are always anxious and pessimistic people who feel that their world is passing through a grave and dangerous crisis. They are numerous today, and this time their fears do seem to be well grounded, for the changes today are so radical as to make one think of the sixteenth century. The evidence for this is there for everyone to see. Since 1850, to take a chance date, scientific discoveries have almost incredibly multiplied, and many of them have been put to such remarkable practical uses that even a Leonardo da Vinci, were he to come to life again, would be unable to believe his senses. Horses, the once inseparable friends of man, have almost vanished from the city streets, cleanliness is now next to godliness, new medical knowledge and drugs have checked diseases and pain, the air is as familiar as land and sea for travel. As a result of new means of communication not only has nearly the whole world been seen and explored, but also distance proves no barrier to conversation. Without calling upon Marshall McLuhan as a witness to a change in our sensibilities, we can see all around us a conformity of techniques so great that one writer has called this world of ours just one technopolis, and races which a generation or two ago were illiterate and looked upon as savages or primitives now have taken on a new look, and are attempting to copy and rival the most up-to-date nations. The world, therefore, is becoming one, economically, socially, perhaps culturally, and as a Teilhard de Chardin liked to think, even religiously. This has never happened before, never even been seriously considered. The change has been described in a phrase by a German theologian, Dietrich Bonhoeffer, a phrase which has caught on—"Man has come of age."

By this Bonhoeffer meant that mankind has passed successively from swaddling clothes, childhood, and adolescence to a stage when he can be independent and look after himself without the need to call upon his gods. Man is now in control of his own destiny. He has an adequate knowledge of his body (if not of his soul), of his private powers, and of a social life which has gradually taken on the shape of a democracy. He is at home with nature at last for he now knows many of its secrets, physical, chemical, and electronic, and can turn them to his own benefit. So much so is this that in many countries people can avoid brute nature in houses artificially warmed, eat artificial food, and can move about safely in machines crammed with protective devices. A degree of security has been reached which mutes fear. Moreover most now can demand their rights and enjoy some liberty.

Such, I think, with legitimate exaggeration, is how modern civilization can be described. Naturally, when men and women have so many opportunities for skilled work, for games, for the arts and leisure, the dream of a perfectly happy human life comes to the surface—in other words, humanism as the epitome and fullness of life. The word itself is associated with the aims and ideals of Renaissance man, though, as may well be supposed, the desire of classical humanism, with its Platonic traditions, held firmly that there was a region of absolute truths, and these truths could be discovered by human reason. This was rationalism built on a rock; but now it seems the rock has worn away and humanism seeks other kinds of support. Not that there is any reversion to religion. Indeed, here the old firm rationalism is still brought to bear to destroy superstitions and myths and to eradicate all that cannot be defended by science. The image of Prometheus challenging and defying the old gods is still popular, and he can be made to represent man having come of age, man emancipated from childish beliefs and now able to create for himself a world of plenty and of peace. Here the humanist and the Communist join hands. The Marxist philosophy predicted the end of conflicts: there would be a short interim after the collapse of capitalism, and then would begin the golden age of the workers of the world united in a classless society. Religion, which served a purpose when men lived in servitude and misery, providing as it did a temporary solace, could have no purpose amongst those who now had all that human freedom could provide. This strong hope inspired the first followers of Marx; but when the down-to-earth Lenin saw that the opposing forces were not likely to collapse within a short space of time, he became more interested in immediate results than in far-off Utopias. The early liberals followed suit. They too had believed in a rapid perfecting of man once his chains were removed but long since they have changed their expectations: and it is this changeover to the practical, and the abandonment of dogmas based on *a priori* reasoning, which characterizes humanism today. The humanist speaks with his ears attentive to what the scientists are saying. Their message is nearly unanimous. Gone is the Victorian confidence in the finality of scientific theories, in the uniformity of nature and the fixed relation of effect to cause. The word "cause" is taboo, and laws of nature now look almost like a hoax. In short scientists now do not concern themselves about the nature of reality: they are content with provisional successes.

This change can be seen very clearly in a book called *Objections to Humanism*.[1] This is a work written by humanists; they frankly state the difficulties in their position as, in a former book, *Objections to Christian Belief*, some leading Christians faced what they felt to be the main difficulties against the Christian religion. In the first-mentioned book a notable antipathy is shown to any form of certitude. I suppose this is partly due to a longstanding unwillingness among English thinkers to bend their heads before any dogma, but it is also an expression of a contemporary attitude.[2] The "democratic social order," writes the editor, H. J. Blackham, "is independent of ultimate (and contentious) beliefs, Christian, humanist or other." The sciences now lean on probability and eschew certainty, and in social life we must be content with rules which rest upon common consent. At the turn of the century the world

[1] Published by Constable in 1964.
[2] Even though the German idealists who followed Kant were very free in their use of words like "absolute," I think, to judge by remarks in philosophic journals, it is the Descartes idea of certainty plus the Victorian assurance about the uniformity of nature and absolute laws of causality which have been uppermost in the minds of the modern philosophers and scientists. To those trained in Aristotle and Plato and the theories of knowledge which stemmed from them it is a matter of extreme surprise that a philosopher like Gilbert Ryle could identify the correspondence view of truth with a one-to-one relationship between the object and the image or idea of it. Still more amazing is it that Wittgenstein, influenced no doubt by Lord Russell, should bother to make an attempt in his *Tractatus Logico-Philosophicus* to work out as in a mosaic bit by bit the truth relation of words to things, a straightforward meaning of the world around us; and when this did not work out, that he should abandon all hope of discovering a truth relationship between the mind and reality.

turned pragmatic, and the United States led the way. It gave a striking example of how to "get on," to make the most of present conditions, and this way of approaching life fitted in with modern scientific methods. Kathleen Nott goes so far as to pretend that the quest for certainty is a neurotic quest for emotional security. The neurotic wants to be relieved from the need of taking personal decisions. This of course is easy to say, but more than difficult to prove. Why not say instead that it is the mark of an adolescent mind to make snap judgments and jump to conclusions like the above? More plausible is her view that the majority of people do not rely on absolutes and cannot follow the old abstract ways of arguing. Miss Nott herself favors a "passive attitude towards experience," one which "unites theory and practice. This makes one concerned not with final or incorrigible statements but with results that work." She regards theological or philosophical debates as usually a battle of wits or prejudices. Each side is out for victory and truth is the first victim. This of course when stated so categorically is nonsense. One has only to read the dialogues of Plato and some of the great historical debates to see the splendor of reasoning; but Miss Nott has in mind the father of much modern philosophy, namely, Descartes. His method and his earnest quest for an indubitable certainty did have an influence and narrowed down the aims of many thinkers who succeeded him. It is attractive to try to find what Descartes set out to find, that is, an immediate, primitive truth, a first starting point. As is well known, he thought he had found it in "I think, therefore I am." Many who have little sympathy with Miss Nott's ideas would agree that this method of Descartes' was a mistaken one. That would not mean that they could tolerate her conclusion, which is a denial that "one can rationally demonstrate the existence of anything."

Kingsley Martin in his essay in the same book is at one with Miss Nott in his depreciation of the old rationalism.

He writes that "the great differences between humanism in the eighteenth century and today are, first, that we no longer believe in a fixed natural law: and, secondly, we have been made aware of the intrusion of the unconscious in our ordinary thinking." Humanists as well as religious moralists in the past have put too much stress on theoretical grounds for their beliefs. Morality does not depend on any set of doctrines: it rests on the basic needs of a civilized society. Evolution is the password in philosophy as in science, and "all fixed authority is a casualty in an evolutionary age." In place therefore of the Platos and Aristotles, the Descartes and the Kants—what Dante calls "the blessing of high thought" (*il ben dell intelletto*)—Kingsley Martin recommends the modern "do-gooder," for today "the concern of thinking people is with the health, wealth and happiness of mankind." If Kingsley Martin were to be taken seriously and literally it would be necessary to watch out for the "intrusion of the unconscious" in all that he is writing. I think, however, one can see without looking to this how bedazzled he is by a word like "evolution" and an expression such as "basic needs."

Mr. Blackham in a concluding essay comments on this terrestrial ideal of Kingsley Martin. He quotes Jefferson's phrase, "happiness on earth and greater happiness hereafter," and adds "that this is a somewhat complacent creed, and not too comforting when the second part of it is omitted." Thoughtfully he points to the persistence down the ages of two "clear-cut themes" of the human situation. One theory accepts or argues that this world is all man has or ever will have, and so he must make the best of it. The other theory has for its key word "pilgrimage." Here in this world we have no lasting home, and we are passing through human life to another kind of existence. Blackham does not take up any decided position himself. In this respect he is one with Miss Nott and Kingsley Martin in refusing to be dogmatic. Let us live, he suggests, without trying to coerce truth to one view or the other, making the best of this world and perhaps entertaining hopes that there may be something better to come.

I have said that these views, which play down the sovereign quality of reason and turn aside from dogma, are in keeping with modern trends, especially perhaps in the fast-moving United States. Mere speculation, it is said, leads into the void, and meantime we can always improve on what we have. This pragmatic philosophy, which never quite convinced an older generation, has now become increasingly popular, and, as we have seen, humanists use its language. But there is another influence equally if not even more strong—what goes by the name of existentialism. It is relatively a newcomer. Most would argue that Kierkegaard is its progenitor. Since his time however the word has been used so loosely that it is not always clear what meaning is intended. Kierkegaard revolted against the conventional Christianity he saw around him in Denmark, and he was gravely disappointed by the idealist, metaphysical philosophies which came from Germany. He felt that there was no life in these abstract ideas which were being mouthed—no lesson for him as a bewildered anxious individual. Nietzsche in a striking sentence summed up the weaknesses of this sort of thinking: philosophers, he said, liked to sit on the steps out of the heat and light of the sun, busily knitting the trousers of the spirit. The revolt against such philosophizing was so strongly felt and so personal that at first it seemed a denial of all theorizing. Its adherents were like Cain, condemned to be "a fugitive and a vagabond" on the face of the earth, having, however, a mark by which they could be recognized. They have, in fact, several marks, including a vivid sense of their own loneliness, a deep concern close to anguish, and an impatience with the limitations of reason. The lack of coherence in existentialist writings at first made it unattractive to the hard thinkers in university circles, especially where there existed a tradition of exact analysis of words and sentences as well as fidelity to logic. But in time, as was bound to happen, existentialists grew into a school with some common features and a countenance which could be described as semiphilosophical. Now, partly owing to its liaison with phenomenology, it has dispossessed some of the more famous systems and everywhere in lecture rooms, in religion and literature its voice can be heard. Such a success must have its reasons. One is a reaction against and dissatisfaction with the failure of the old philosophies to give a lead. More immediate is, I think, a sense, already mentioned, of being of age. Coming of age brings with it a realization of one's own claims and responsibilities—the responsibility, for instance, of playing one's part in society and of coming to terms with one's self. And it is just here that the *juventus mundi* finds itself so hard hit. The growth of technical knowledge and of mass production crushes the individual. It may well be that in a modern society where ciphers and computers, IBM cards, vast stores, trades unions, state and borough regulations, and state controls and military service prevail, the longing grows to be able to express, even in some wild way, personal feelings, hopes, loves, and disgusts. The beatniks and the hippies, the habit of drug taking, represent the queer side of the existentialist psychology.

We might add to this, I think, that in an urban and utilitarian society, *pace* Harvey Cox, the pragmatist may be in demand, but he is a dull fellow and has a bourgeois strut to his bank or many-floored department. The existentialist is at one with the utilitarian in finding little use for theoretical talk, for metaphysics or dogmas, but he is more interested in those activities of the self which have been submerged in the rushing current of day-to-day life. Not buying and selling nor abstruse theories on "the thing in itself" concern him, but rather the underground roots of the self, its isolation and desire to communicate, its authenticity and commitment, its hope and its despair. The Reverend Martyn

Thornton in *The Rock and the River* describes existentialism as "an approach to the problems of life streaming from the uncertainty and instability of the world scene, which expresses itself in the rejection of metaphysics and idealism in favour of the personal and practical." This is a contemporary judgment which marks one definite change from the views of Kierkegaard. Kierkegaard has been an inspiration to many Christians in different countries and of different creeds. His problems were basically religious, and it was his rejection of the worldly ideas of the Churchmen around him and their low-toned convictions which led him to set faith outside all reasoning. It meant a leap in the dark, a walking on waters like that of St. Peter "five thousand fathoms deep" to reach the outstretched arms of the Lord Jesus. In Martyn Thornton's account existentialism has become secular.

Now it might be thought that a view which came so near to despair of human nature could not in any straightforward sense of the word be called "humanistic." It certainly does not tune in with the Renaissance belief in the beauty of human nature. Nevertheless it does introduce a new motif or theme without which humanism would be incomplete. That this is so is shown by the development of existentialism this last hundred years, a development which has been fairly consistent and has ended in philosophies such as those of Sartre, Gabriel Marcel, and Heidegger, which have proved to be happy hunting grounds for the humanists. Heidegger, I own, does not like to be labeled, and he distinguishes between two senses and spellings of the word "existential." "Existential" in his vocabulary refers to our human condition in time and space, long before we can make decisions as to how we shall create ourselves. From his birth each person is a live member of a community which molds him or her in a contemporary way. Shakespeare could not be a Dante—neither in physique nor in his politics or social outlook nor in cultural habits.

The second meaning, which is differentiated from the first by the spelling "existentiell," refers to what we can do ourselves with the physical and psychical constitution it is our fate to be given. That is, we have to adorn the Sparta which has been assigned to us. Freedom is the mark of a person, and we start as incomplete persons, who gradually by our own efforts come to make a personal center of ourselves. Our encounter with others and our right choices are the means whereby we do this.

In developing these views Heidegger does in fact sketch anew the properties and ideals of a human person. He corrects the image of the individual man with which Descartes started. For the latter the "I" is cut off from all else and uncertain of everything. Moreover he is a ghost in the machine. Heidegger discusses this unnatural posture of the ego, realizing that there is no thought, no understanding of the self without the accompanying knowledge of others and a world around. We are not coldly watching spectators of a scene alien to the self; we are more like one of a shoal of fish wriggling in a net. Being human our individual life is also a racial affair. That is why we can contemplate a humanistic ideal. What then is peculiar to the existentialist approach as studied in Heidegger's writings? Like Kierkegaard and others, he looks at the self in its private history with the magnifying glass of phenomenologists such as Husserl. This privacy, however, clearly goes with teamwork, and this being-with-others creates in us "concern." Then just because we are not things, but persons responsible for ourselves as free, we have to face reality and not run away from it into a sham world of our own makebelieve. That is, we have to be "authentic." We must take up our cross, the cross of our unfortunate heritage, unfortunate in that we start so weak and unsure, and all ends in death, the *coup de grâce* to all our striving. What does nevertheless lie within our power is to act worthily of our freedom, live a truly personal life, and give a use and meaning to all that is bound up with us. In so doing we create a world of values, express a reputable humanity, and transcend the apparent limits of our being.

This estimate of life would not appeal even to the Knight of the Dolorous Countenance; the note of death is too insistent. In the midst of death, however, there is a genuine humanistic appeal to fair behavior, to concern and affection and to the will to live by commitment, encounter, and ensuing authenticity. Kierkegaard might well have been put off by the metaphysical and mystagogic style of Heidegger, but what is a stumbling block becomes in the writings of Sartre an exciting canter. The existentialist and humanist outlook is perhaps more suited to plays and novels, and Sartre can make us realize, as the prophet Nathan did King David, that we who read are ourselves the subjects and victims analyzed by existentialist and phenomenological philosophers. We are listening to our story, to the plight we are in, one and all.

It is in the writings of Sartre more than in Heidegger that we hear the voice of Prometheus. Prometheus, who defied the gods, stole (their) fire, and is the patron of secular humanism. Neither Heidegger nor Sartre brings God into the picture. Sartre, however, is much more explicit in his atheism: Heidegger makes cryptic remarks about periods when God is absent. Existentialism is, I think, really neutral on the question of theism. It made its name as a secularist philosophy, but its theme can be illustrated by quotation after quotation from the Psalms, and Christians of all denominations have associated themselves with it. The Protestant finds it a more up-to-date way of playing on the harp of religious experience, while among certain Catholics it too is a pet way of absolving themselves from reading the heavier volumes of St. Thomas. An outstanding figure, Gabriel Marcel, does not swear by the words of any master, but he has affinities to the existentialists. He is existentialist, humanist, and Christian all in one, because of his openness and sympathy with his fellow men. His humanistic creed comes in short to this: Being is not a subject one can question or argue about (antimetaphysical); it is there; it is a mystery and not a problem (Gabriel-Marcellian). I have no possible existence outside being: nevertheless I confront being and I am always "in a situation" (existentialist). In "this situation" I can distinguish between what I am and what I have, and I can get rid of what I have, but I cannot get rid of myself. This distinction between having and being forms the warp and woof of Marcel's meditations, and it also prepares us for his brand of humanism. The distinction resembles that of Martin Buber between the I-It and the I-Thou. In loving authentically and resisting the temptation to treat all we meet as things and so possess them, we find a world opening out to us. If we continue faithful and loyal to this insight and put ourselves at others' dispositions, we come to a true sense of self and of others, enter into personal relationships of infinite value, and finally we invoke One who is beyond all I am and have. This engages us in an act of faith in God. In contrast with Sartre, who, when presented with the human situation, the spawning ugliness of it all, has a feeling of nausea, Marcel is conscious of an affinity with the world he meets. Optimistically he adopts an attitude of goodwill to it which he finds is justified by its results. He extends his arms and makes himself generously open to experience. As a result his humanism acts as a kind of witness to the possibility of a good life and of a religious encounter when faith begins a new life of love.

All these views which I have so far mentioned have this in common, that they make human beings the touchstone of their theories and keep away from the world of essences and categories in which former philosophers were wont to take delight. These good men and true used for weapons syllogisms and mathematical symbols, predicates and predicaments, genera and species, and they pursued their abstractions into regions where no human footprint could ever be found. Their El Dorado was essence, the essence or nature of reality. Their search being thought unrewarding, the thinkers who descend from Kierkegaard have given it up and turned to existence, to what we can feel and touch and experience—our own felt experience and our personal relations with others. We hear much now of the value of dialogue and participation. This approach leads straight to some form of humanism, for we can give a far more prepossessing account of what a man is than in the old tomes. There we read that man was a rational animal or an emanation of the One or a ghost in the machine; but now man's face is being drawn with his lovable features as well as his warts. Even with God, if it be permitted to say anything about Him, His countenance becomes more human, more recognizable, let us say, than in a Cubist abstraction.

Those in the theist camp who are in sympathy with the more pragmatic thought of today see it as an advance on the past and a correction of some of its arid concepts. Now if this claim were justified we would have ready and prepared for us the right procedure for assessing Christian humanism. When, however, we look more closely at what this new type of Catholic theologian is saying, his assertiveness gives us pause. A favorite technique of his is to compare the new with the past in terms of the fresh and topical as against the static and out of date. Indeed this sharp distinction between static and dynamic ideas is a key one. The argument runs that with one great exception, past writers had no sense of history or development in ideas. They were as philosophers preoccupied with the idea of necessity and with eternal essences. Until the late eighteenth century or early nineteenth century, man and nature were thought of as fixed and unchanging. The ancients were fascinated by the unchanging seven wonders of the world, by the Egyptian pyramids, the everlasting hills. They saw the sun rise and set, and concluded that the same sun was ever returning. The moralists, for their part, regarded the natural law as unchanging, and believed that the barbarians and the most remote peoples of the earth would be in their moral views as like the Stoics or a Grotius as two peas. Each species remained intact and separate from another, and man had a nature or essence which could be described in exact philosophical language. This attitude lasted through the centuries, and it was not modified or abandoned until evolution captivated men's minds. Already before Darwin, Hegel had guessed that "becoming" was a better name for what was happening than "being," and he built his whole system on this supposed truth. The idea caught on, and science in a very different field confirmed it. Nowadays "history," which once was as despised as an unskilled workingman, is a kind of grand vizier. Everyone has to pay attention to it, for "all ideas must be looked at historically."

In a review of Anatole France in *The Times Literary Supplement* (September 29, 1966), "the present age" is described as "Dionysiac not Olympian. We take human existence, human dignity, commitment and a host of other semi-religious concepts very solemnly, and if anyone does not accept our views we take him into the mountains and rend him to pieces." Catholic writers, it must be confessed, have joined this Bacchanalian throng. The distinguished theologian Fr. Bernard Lonergan, S.J., calls this change now occurring one from classicism to historical consciousness (*Existenz und Aggiornamente, Focus 2,* 1965). What precisely he means by "historical consciousness" I am not quite sure, for history without permanent landmarks and criteria gives no basis for any worthwhile historical judgment. Objective evidence, too, must be there to give subjective norms some degree of validity. Charles Davis, who has quoted Fr. Lonergan, does try to make clear what "historical consciousness" means. In the *Clergy Review* (August 1966) he says that "Classicism regards man as a nature already defined and essentially unchanging, and objective truth as fixed in unchanging concepts outside the mind. Historical consciousness sees man as a person or subject in a process of becoming. Man's being is a becoming for which he is responsible, and community as properly human is made by his freedom. Objective truth is a function of developing mind and is always marked by historicity." Now this unfortunately looks to be a *lucus a non lucendo*, because the language is so lacking in exactness. What, for instance, could an unchanging concept be which exists fixed "outside the mind"? A concept is a mental construction and it may or may not be true of the reality of which it is meant to be a concept. Again, if we are to see a man "as a person or subject in a process of becoming," we are bound to ask, becoming what? The only possible answer we can give is, becoming a person or a more developed man. This means that there is all the time a being who is becoming himself, that is to say, a stable being. So either Davis is uttering a tautology or he is saying the opposite of what he wants to say. A static, stable being has stuck his head out. The same result follows if we analyze the sentence: "Man's being is a becoming for which he is responsible." Who is this "he" who is responsible? It cannot be the "becoming" for he is responsible for it. So it looks as if there is a "being" all the time whose existence is not covered by calling him a "becoming" *tout court*. Lastly, Davis tells us that "objective truth is a function of developing mind." I think this is meant to bring out an important truth, to wit, that it takes time to see aspects of a truth so that we are constantly growing in our appreciation of it and of what it entails. There is, then, a progression in our understanding of certain truths, and as this progression is temporal, history as an ordered account of human behavior and ideas has a function not to be neglected. There are, however, truths and truths, and there are certain elementary truths which do not grow in the same way as our knowledge of revealed religious doctrines which have normally some mystery attached to them; or again, historical truths themselves, consciousness of ourselves and others, seem to follow a special law of growth. So, too, certain fundamental human relationships, such as motherhood or companionship, love and hate, seem to remain relatively unchanged. There is no historical law forcing us to believe that Socrates knew less about right and good than we do; and even if we believed Christ to be no more than a man, it could still be maintained that he had deeper insights and was more high-minded than any other hero of our Western civilization. All this goes, I think, to show that Davis is rash in writing of objective truth as a function of developing mind. Many will have the uncomfortable thought that if this is all that objective truth means, then truth is not objective at all.

All of us must admit, nevertheless, that there has been a change in outlook and in insight into certain types of truths. The problem is to what extent this change modifies what is called the old "static" view, and secondly, whether existentialism or pragmatism gives a correct interpretation of this change. As we have already seen, contrasts are now constantly made between essences and existence, being and becoming, and one form of this contrast is shown in the quotation already given about "classicism" and the "historical consciousness," or in other terms between "static" and "dynamic" truth. These various distinctions may not all have the same import, and so one has to beware of the transference of an adjective from a context where it is legitimate to another in which it has no proper bearing. Essentialism is what Kierkegaard loathed, the inhuman, as he thought it, engrossment in what is generic, universal, merely conceptual. The absent-minded philosopher is an object of laughter, if not ridicule. He is up in a balloon or always looking for his spectacles. Nietzsche summed up this attitude when he wrote that "a married philosopher belongs to comedy." This kind of criticism does show how hard it is to be a philosopher and a full human being at the same time, and it may be that in any humanistic Utopia those with the highest tasks, the philosopher, the priest and monk, the statesman and artist, will be conspicuous for their limitations as well as for their special virtues. We do, in fact, owe so much to the ancient philosophers for drawing back the curtains of the world; the one showing the unchanging stillness of reality, the second its constant flow, and a third the pure world, yonder, of forms. So wonderful was this world of pure forms to Plato that he relegated this world of ours of sense experience to a condition like that of a moving waste of waters, and made the forms, beauty, truth, and goodness, and kindred spiritual shapes to be unchanging and everlasting like the stars at night. So acceptable was this view that the belief in the unchanging character of truth prevailed until the nineteenth century. We have seen how and when evolution brought a different conception of truth, which has affected science as well as philosophy.

Its effect upon Catholic philosophy and theology was slower. Étienne Gilson was one of the first, if not the first to loosen the views of St. Thomas Aquinas from the too close links with Aristotle. He argued that the Thomistic system was not one made up of logical necessities like that of Plotinus or Spinoza or even Aristotle. At the head and at the end of the system was the concept of a living God. God is not the ground of being or reality from which one can deduce all that is contained within being or reality—that would be talking in terms of necessity and essence. God is the loving Creator of a world independent of Himself, a world of things and a world of free persons. These free persons will find their final bliss in union with this same living God, a union in which human personality will still persist, for "He is thy being but thou not his" (*Epistle of Privy Counsel*). This interpretation of Gilson's is of topical importance, but it cannot be said that Thomistic philosophy has been a factor in the changeover to the modern existential dynamic attitude. It is more probable that this approach made Thomistic scholars think again about the metaphysics of St. Thomas and reform their views. Duns Scotus is probably nearer to the modern in his insistence on will as against intellect, and on individuality as against species or genus. Duns Scotus, however, was a wholehearted metaphysician, and metaphysics is the *bête noire* of the modern, so perhaps for precursors we should look to the reformers of the Renaissance, who worked to ostracize metaphysics because it froze the loving experience man should have of God.

This supposed opposition between essence and existence which for the time being has ended in the victory of the latter may seem to some only very distantly related to what is meant by existentialism or the dynamics of the "historical consciousness." There are differences, certainly, which must not be forgotten, but I think they all fall within the pattern of modern life and must have a say in the kind of humanism which is in men's minds—as peace, also, is an object of immediate desire and hope. The chief modern idea, which is an ideal as well, revolves round that of a person, his claims to liberty, fraternity, and equality, and how he can express and fulfill his individual life. In earlier times stories were about the deeds of heroes, and even in the great novels of the nineteenth century the main interest often was in the drama of man against fate or circumstances or evil men. Gradually narrative has become more and more psychological, the dissection of human motives or purely sexual ones, and the clash of them in marriage or politics or war. Biographies, autobiographies, and memoirs pour out from the printing presses. Most universities now have a chair or faculty of psychology, experimental and scientific as well as psychoanalytical. Art has moved away from content and representative work to the symbolic and subjective. So it is no wonder if a philosophy has developed which has for its foremost interest the human self.

This human self has now all the stage lights concentrated on it, and is the special preserve of the existentialists. But it may still be asked, what has all this to do with the philosophical distinction of essence and existence and the interest in humanism. In philosophy the word "existent" is usually synonymous with actual. When Achilles cried that it were better to be alive than a strengthless shade he was clinging to existence. So, too, many proverbs and sayings bring out the importance of distinguishing between an idea and its actualization. The man dying of hunger dreams of food, but dreams of food do not save a life. The well-known ontological argument for the existence of God as formulated by St. Anselm and then by Descartes and Leibniz turns on this very distinction, whether there is one exception to the rule, namely, God. God being the most perfect being conceivable, He must exist, for a being conceived and existing is more perfect than a being merely conceived. The philosophers tell us that to say a thing or person exists does not tell us any more about the thing or person. Caesar alive and Caesar dead have the same nature. That is why it makes no difference in what one writes about Caesar, or, for that matter, a Neanderthal man or an ichthyosaurus. Nevertheless, as the famous line "To be or not to be" shows, to exist is the crowning act and without it there is nothing left but what might be, a world of possibilities. But existence by itself is even more empty. Hence though we have to distinguish essence and existence, they needs must travel together like Siamese twins.

Were this all, then the relation between the philosophical use of the word "existence" and what the existentialists mean by it would seem very tenuous. But there is a connecting link and one which helps to explain why both uses have become of contemporary interest. Existentialists profess to ignore essences. Sartre, for instance, admits the presence of an *en soi*—a thing in itself—but holds that human beings can never attain the status of an *en soi*. But in fact he calls-the human self a *pour soi,* it is a semi-real longing in vain to be a full self, and this is really an admission that he is thinking of the peculiar nature of a human being, which is both real and nevertheless capable of becoming more fully real by its own free efforts. Sartre goes on to use the word "authentic" of this kind of being. This word serves to ensure that we are talking about the genuine article and not *ersatz* material. Cases in point would be whether we possessed a genuine Stradivarius or a true first-century papyrus, or butter and not margarine. This, however, is only a secondary use of the word "authentic" because so far I have been writing about objects with genuine or fake essences and not of their existence. But already here perhaps the language seems unreal, because we might ask, "Is that actually a Stradivarius?" as a child might ask of an object in its hand, "Is this an actual leprechaun?" It is when we come to persons that we come upon "existence" in its new meaning. I shall have more to say later on the double sense which philosophers like Heidegger have clamped onto the word. For the moment it is sufficient to point to the peculiar constitution of a person. A human person is aware of himself, aware that he is on the brink of nothingness, that death will blot him out, that he is responsible for what he is and what he will become; and so he is a creature with *sorge* and anguish and power of choice, standing off from himself and therefore ex-istant.

The connection and difference between these new and old senses of existence is, I hope, now clear. The old philosophers placed man in the universe one amongst other beings, a kind of Adam in Paradise, naming objects around him. The distinctions they made held for all known objects in the universe, and so it was left to a sophisticated, self-conscious, and unhappy generation to emphasize man's strange fate of being self-conscious, lonely, and with bad dreams. One must not, however, exaggerate here. Existence, as hinted above, has been used in a sense which brings out man's contingency, frailty, vulnerability. We do not usually say of a person that he exists; instead we say that he is alive. We can point at him or meet him. But if he dies, that is the end and no more can be said. Indeed death tells us quite simply by its finality all that we lose in being alive. "The shield of Saul fallen on Mount Gilboa, bright once with oil, will never be seen again. . . . Saul and Jonathan more lovely and pleasant in their lives, and in their death they were not divided." Here we see existence and life as one. To David, Saul was such a warrior, so virile, that he could not think of him dead. From this the mind moves on to an ultimate connection between life and existence, to an idea of life as being so strong as to be incapable of extinction. The feeling for that is in the legend of Achilles, who had only one spot in his body that was vulnerable. Even a child would see that it was hard to kill an angel, and so strong is this belief in the resistance to death of spirit that primitive peoples and civilized alike allow for its immortality. So we see that if we substitute the word "life" for "existence" in writing of human beings, the distinction between nature and essence and existence diminishes and points to a unique kind of life in which they would be so inseparable as to appear identical. For this reason, among others, the existentialists are justified in attempting a fresh philosophy of the human person, a philosophy which leads straight on to a critique of humanism. That this is so is well shown in an article by the Reverend Leo Sweeney in *The New Scholasticism* (Vol. XI, January 1966). "The leading Existentialists," he writes, "such as Heidegger, Jaspers, Sartre and Marcel, concentrate on man and specifically on his human condition." Their verdict is that "only men, only subjects are real, in the sense of intrinsically and *per se* being perfect, valuable, significant, and that what makes them alone be real is the fact that they are men, they are subjects. Primacy is not rooted in their actuality but in their humanity, their subjectivity. A philosophical position which insists upon a primacy so conceived is a humanism, a philosophy of subjectivity, a philosophy of essence, to use Marcel's own phrase, an essentialism, since reality is viewed as flowing from what human existents are and not the fact that they are."

This looks topsy-turvy and not all that is said about subjectivity may be acceptable, but the conclusion is clear, namely, that existentialism does not rely so exclusively on the existential side as to exclude essence, and therefore it does and should parade itself as a form of humanism. That leading existentialists take up a severe moral attitude is further evidence for this. Moreover we learn that it demands of all that they should meet the challenge of the human situation and make themselves centers of initiative and free collaboration with others. In so doing they become authentically human. In elaborating this idea they warn us all that we have an enemy within us who tempts us to inertia, to accept conventional standards and become like Kipling's *Tomlinson*, without a soul of our own. An opponent of theirs with some justification could claim that they are inconsistent, that they are trying to have their cake and eat it. They have poured scorn on conceptual schemes and on the rationalisms of the past. They use new slogans, bidding us live by our free will alone and the experiences associated with the will, that is, creative personal acts, encounters with others, and total commitment in a dialogue of love. Those were enough to give life zest and opportunity despite a cosmic meaninglessness and the menace of death. But they leap over the wall of partition and share many ideas with those they repudiate. This being so, it can be argued that theirs is not such an extreme view after all; it is merely that they have turned left instead of right in the same motorcar on a road said to be a dead end. This is important, for it means that the existentialists have, in order to define and sharpen their point of view, created opponents who are imaginary men of straw, whereas in fact, like certain advertising agencies, they are giving new names to the same old medicines.[3] Did Marcel let the cat out of the bag when he called his own view a "philosophy of essence"? It is true that Marcel does not rank himself among the existentialists, but his approach with its side-stepping of the Scholastics' systematic rationalism is in many respects like that of Sartre and Camus. The present generation of writers, religious and nonreligious, are over-excitedly aware of the crisis of the present age—its almost eschatological character and alienation from the past as "a thousand years removed thing" and feel that they are diagnosing rightly the spirit dominating the present age. This diagnosis is of the kind I have already described, where the dynamic is opposed to the static and becoming to being; existential and situational answers must supersede the old ones, which have remained always broadly the same. They dispense with a rational approach in order to make a personal appeal and take a more personal oath of allegiance.

Some conservatives see good only in the past, and now, en revanche, they are ignored by the liberals and existentialists who can think of little else than their own contemporary spiritual aches and hampered freedom. The Marxists have their own explanation of history and of the service done by religion when the world was young. There are plenty who dislike communism, who will, all the same,

[3] In a recent book, called The Reactionaries, Mr. John Harrison discusses, as if it were a serious puzzle, whether D. H. Lawrence, T. S. Eliot, Wyndham Lewis, and Yeats were fascists. I am sorry to say too that Sir Karl Popper in his Open Society marks Plato and Hegel with the same brand. In a like manner but worse, Rolf Hochhuth in his plays can brand Pope Pius XII, Winston Churchill, Lord Cherwell, and Dr. Bell, the former Bishop of Chichester. The damning description by existentialists and avant-garde Catholics of many distinguished past philosophers and theologians when they are called dogmatists with static ideas belongs to the same kind of syndrome. As Father Coughlin and Joe McCarthy smelt Communists everywhere, so a certain perfervid type of democrat has to make emotional noises and label those who do not agree with him fascists.

agree that metaphysics is a game played by adolescents. As in literature and drama the first imaginative pictures and concerts are of the mythical wonders of the universe, so with vasty cosmic systems and patterns. Later comes the poise of mind still relatively untroubled, and only at the end does the reflection of Minerva turn fully within and dwell on the scourge of living, loneliness, and the death in life. The day has come for modern psalms *à la De Profundis,* for Rimbaud's "Sometimes a drowning man descends half-dreaming," for a Ulysses, who makes his Odyssey amid the strange islands and storms of the conscious and subconscious.

> Defeats on them like leaves
> Have fallen, fell, kept falling, fell
> On them, poor lovies.
> (WYSTAN HUGH AUDEN)

Were this so, the moderns would be their own undertakers. More soberly and sensibly, others try to bring the past and present together. What now seems new is, it is said, only new as the light changes the color of the rose or the dancers in a theater. Each generation in a period of culture has the truth, but not wholly. It experiences all that is truly human, but selects what is relevant to its own problems with only a glance at the rest—as in a multitude of faces we pick out those of friends and enemies. But while there is no deficiency in human experience when human beings are sufficiently grown up to look around and look after themselves, there are of course vast changes in knowledge due to new data, new interests, methods, and new discoveries. New data do not, however, of themselves make us more human. One can be as human on a horse or in a horse-drawn coach as in a motorcar. There have been saints, virtuous men and women, and wise ones throughout history and irrespective of the times they have been living in. And yet civilizations develop and we sit on the shoulders of the past and can gain from their mistakes and utilize their hints. At the very center, however, of all this discussion of growth is our power to improve upon what is already known. Here by "known" I am not referring to the way in which the discoveries of steam and electricity, for example, lead on from the simplest kind of engine to the modern beautiful monsters—the plane of a Wilbur Wright changing beyond all belief to a supersonic giant. All that kind of progress is easily explicable, though one wonders why the genius who discovered the steam engine could not foresee some of the developments. This is a conundrum analogous to why athletes can keep on breaking records. One asks how long they can go on doing this, and whether there be a definite limit somewhere, say, for the mile or high jump.

What concerns us here, however, is the development of common ideas and truth. Man has always had some idea of change and development. He has seen change all around him, water freezing, the sun drying clothes, food cooked and eaten, and for development there is that of children into men, and, as in the fairy tale, ugly ducklings turning into snow-white swans. It is not then the knowledge of change which is new, but the explanation of it. In past times, let it be granted, critics and writers and theologians especially, impressed by the apparent unchanging character of so much in nature and in ideals and in morals, were led to pin down the objects they were considering, label them, and, as a result, underrate the importance of change. This habit was strengthened by another—one very human and strong—namely, to ignore small changes until, for instance, a tire bursts or a button comes off one's coat. As Bergson pointed out, we cannot work with a constant *élan vital:* we cut up the flow of time into minutes, and in our own case and with others into birthdays. This procedure works with most objects of our senses, but a special problem arises with objects of the spirit. We happen on a truth—at school, for example, when painstakingly we learn sums in mathematics—or in a thought-out conclusion, or in a vivid intuition. There is a finality in truth which makes us wish to put a colophon on the concluding page. When Archimedes cried out "Eureka" on discovering the principle of specific gravity, I am sure he felt that he had completed a piece of knowledge. So too the early Fathers of the Church at the great councils when they defined the consubstantiality of the Son with the Father and the two natures in Jesus Christ thought that they had settled these questions once and for all. Nevertheless these defined doctrines can without loss to their meaning increase in significance. A modern theologian, such as Karl Rahner, says that a definition is a beginning and not an end—a somewhat unfortunate description because it seems to suggest that we can start all over again with a defined doctrine, as if nothing had already been properly stated. For those who believe that God Himself revealed these doctrines, enlightening us as to His loving intentions toward us, there can be sifting but no changing of this defined sense. If once they become human documents, open to various senses according to the mind of a particular generation or culture, the certainty of God's own word would be compromised, and Christianity would be no better than many another man-made creed. Hence perhaps the care theologians used in accepting any development. They played for safety by allowing only for logical deductions or implications from the original statement. Newman was one of the first to suggest boldly other ways of development, and it is the gravamen of the modern theologian that this old theory was based on a static view of truth, whereas now we know it to be dynamic.

If we examine the history of religious thought and rely on its evidence, what is unmistakable is the clash of ideas rather than a serene unfolding. Catholic theologians have been forced to clarify their own doctrines by the criticism of them by opponents. This is obvious in the matter of the Eucharist as sacrament and sacrifice. It is even obvious in the matter of faith itself. At the Reformation, Luther and other reformers argued that the act of faith was one of trust, a surrender to the loving mercies of God in Christ. It had little or nothing to do with reason. The Catholics resisting such an explanation naturally sought to show its intellectual side—how indeed it was wholly reasonable. Both sides were stimulated to make their views convincing and this led to an increase of information and knowledge about the nature of faith. Only within the last few decades have the two sides drawn nearer, the Protestants accepting an element of reason and the Catholics an element of will and love. Once the latter had recognized this, they began to see that in earlier statements love was accepted as an ingredient, and St. Thomas had explicitly mentioned the will. Two conclusions can be drawn from this one example. The first is that sometimes if not always the end result of a controversy or of some hard new thinking is a more enlightened understanding of what was the Christian teaching through the ages. The new truth was there half-hidden all the time.[4] The second conclusion, and one to which I attribute the most importance, is that knowledge evolves through disputes or put-up resistances to its truth. The Marxist calls this "dialectic," borrowing the idea from Hegel. As, however, dialectic ought really to be reserved for the method of learning by means of question and answer or to the special uses of the word by Plato, Hegel, and Marx, I prefer a more general word which applies to nature as well as to human life and experience, a word such as "tension" or "friction." We have the example of cymbals clashing and making music, and what Dean Inge called the rubbing of the hair of a dead horse over the guts of a dead cat to produce the Ninth Violin Sonata of Beethoven.

[4] Most older writers will, I expect, have had the experience of looking back on youthful work and finding there ideas, in an inchoate form and not reflected upon, which they thought that they had only recently discovered.

The Protestants on the other hand, though they too have had their disputes, were not ridden with as tight a rein as the Catholics, and so their development allowed for such a liberty of interpretation of the Christian faith that it roused reactions, of which the best known is that of Karl Barth. Barth, in his first volumes, would not allow a single breath of human interpretation to blur the Word of God. He and others like-minded do not believe that this liberal theologizing is in any legitimate sense a development of divine truth. He therefore would take the Word of God without testing it by any human, personal experience, rational or historical. The modern philosopher and theologian, however, who has benefited from studying the existentialists and pragmatists, does not, in his own view, belong to the category of the nineteenth-century liberals against whom Barth protests. He is far less confident of the adequacy of reason, and where it is a matter of doctrine he is all for a personal and situational approach. At the best he is for dynamic action, for translating the old into terms relevant to the deep concerns of the present. Later I will give one or two conspicuous examples of how this is to be done. The genuine existentialist has, however, made the task very difficult for himself. Felt interior experience is notoriously difficult to put into words, and were it not that there is already a vast literature to fall back upon, he would be almost speechless. As examples of this literature the Psalms can be quoted: "I am like a pelican of the wilderness . . . and am as a sparrow alone upon the housetop . . . My days are like a shadow that declineth" (Psalm 101); or Jeremias, even Aeschylus and Vergil, St. Augustine and Pascal. These are masters of the diary of the soul, but they are not tied down by any rule limiting their means of expression. The existentialist, on the other hand, has cut off his head and has to listen to the voice of a dead Orpheus as he is carried down the stream. The cardinal words they do use fail to carry all the meanings they wish to convey. "Encounter," for instance, does express certain forms of communication and relationship between human beings, but is like a hobbledehoy when used for the love of a Romeo and Juliet or the ecstasy described in *The Phoenix and the Turtle*. Naturally, then, when they do write on the subjects dear to their hearts, they use their heads more than they have a right to do. Their serious works and novels and plays presuppose so much that goes beyond the range of an existentialist program. Thus Sartre has much to say on freedom and the self, and rightly sees the intimate connection between the two, but I doubt if he is not thinking in conceptualist terms half the time and then corrects himself by a private view of his own which is not borne out by experience. He holds, for example, that we may perform the act continuously of stepping back (*se reculer*) and then going forward with a new answer. He ignores here the strength of habit which makes simple people and fathers of families say the same thing over and over again, not to mention men of determined convictions like his countryman, General de Gaulle. Sartre sticks to his own view and is consistent because he has identified free will and person, and as a result leaves out that slow process in which we develop willpower and by self-denial become masters in our own domain.

Many more objections could be launched against the main positions of existentialism, but I hope enough has been said to show that it has not the wherewithal of itself to give us a complete and rounded form of humanism. It has a "lean and hungry look"; it is full of humanity, not humanism. It presents a man dying on a cross, but without any saving grace. The intellect is fatally absent. Ultimately, despite all its dryness, despite, too, its so often disappointing results, the intellect must have the last say. It alone knows the direction we must take; it alone can keep the middle of the road and save us from falling into a ditch.[5] By itself it is such a plodder—except where love and knowledge coin-

[5] Give Thou my reason that instructive flight
Whose weary wings may on Thy hands still light
(SIR THOMAS BROWNE)

cide—that every now and again there are strikes and petty and serious rebellions. Through the centuries there are outbursts of enthusiasm, they flare into the sky and die out. Men and women are carried away by the excitements of sense or passion, as today thousands of the young take to marijuana or LSD and dream of Utopias and life in a Lotus land. Ronald Knox and many other writers have given us pictures of the various enthusiasms, religious and mystical, social and aesthetic. Feelings and emotions are indispensable blessings, but since the work of Freud and Jung and others they are bound often to be suspect. Moreover it may happen some day—so rapidly now is knowledge of the working of the brain and the nervous system and the glands advancing—that it will be possible to reproduce at will some of these emotions. In recent years parts of the brain hitherto inaccessible have been reached which are the material sources of animals' emotions, such as fear, joy, distress, and hatred. New hearts can be made, and it is claimed that in time new brains may be produced. Such possibilities mean that we can and must put a question mark after the claims of those who rely on their emotional life. But there is one capacity which enables scientists to tell us truly of the significance of their work, a capacity which cannot be radically affected by physical or biological science without science itself committing suicide, and that is our reason. By reason I mean that power within us which can distinguish between what is false and what is true. By it we are able to think logically and scientifically discover facts, verify hypotheses, weigh evidence, know that we are thinking and what we are thinking about, and come to understand ourselves, others, the world, and something about God. It is therefore our one sure safeguard, more than a Horatius at the bridge, the infallible watcher who can test all who approach in the name of truth; the detector, for instance, of the worth of our moral feelings, emotional affections, and dislikes, and even the felt ecstatic rush of certainty that seems at first to be so unquestionably right.

Now reason, like manna and water, is a poor diet for the soul if we have to live on it alone. But, of course, that is not true; we are not machines or computers. It could never give us by itself all that is required for a humanistic ideal. As human beings we can fortunately act truly and lovingly at the same time, and normally as human beings we act like an orchestra, with senses, imagination, memory, emotions, and reason all playing their part. A wise man can make free of his feelings, he can anticipate the slow conclusions of reason by an act of foresight which is almost an intuition. Love indeed can run ahead and signal to reason far behind, and deep affection draws reason along with it and keeps us loyal and steadfast when appearances tempt us to distrust. Furthermore there is a quick virginal type of mind, the Lady and the Unicorn in one, which exorcizes confusion and hate, and when it is seen in the genius, be he mathematician or artist or saint, it makes all the sons of the morning shout for joy.

This apologia for reason is directed not only against existentialism, but also against the prevailing spirit of today. If we turn to the chief commentators of the news and views of today, we will find that while they part company from those who are hostile to reason, they give it only a grudging acknowledgment. Such in America are the modern pragmatists, many of them followers of Dewey, and with them are joined, in most parts of the western hemisphere, the positivists who admire empirical science and deride metaphysics and all absolutes. As already pointed out, current ideas are expressed by modern humanists on the basis of a pragmatic philosophy. What these humanists are saying is constantly reiterated in the statements which appear in newspapers, journals, historical and scientific books. And yet, were there no fixed truths they would be as those who write on water. We walk in the midst of certainties—taking for granted our bodies and their contacts with what is not ourselves—knowing the difference between quantity and quality, high and low, far and near, past and present and future. We have all day long direct experience and immediate memories, and we can name many objects, living and nonliving, which are distinct. Everything we do depends upon thousands and thousands of tiny truths more intricate than the cells of the brain. The modern historical scholar can proudly produce evidence for his conclusions, but there is no need for him to enumerate the science of signs, the growth of the alphabet, the justification of printing, of authorship, of translation, and innumerable other facts which support unmentioned the specific arguments he is using. Immediate evidence accounts for very little of our knowledge. Even if we are stay-at-homes we do not doubt the existence of a Rhodesia or Hong Kong, and we would not normally mistake the Pacific for the Atlantic or think it worthwhile to refute the statement that the play *Hamlet* was not written by Shakespeare but by Canute, King of Denmark and England. The past rises up before us, sometimes shadowy because of the poverty or diversity of the evidence, but at other times as clear as the water pouring over Niagara Falls.

I grant that many of the certainties mentioned are of facts, and many would allow that we can be sure of some of them, facts about our own existence, the name of the town we are living in, reflective knowledge, and awareness of aches and pains. Those, however, who are rigorous in these matters may refer to the Heisenberg Principle of Uncertainty, and maintain that though macro-event knowledge can be as steady as an Egyptian pyramid, we cannot accurately observe micro events. Our observation and experimenting are bound to disturb them. One answer to this is that "macro events" is a quantitative way of stating what may be a highly organized and qualified unity, and as such, truth is to be found in the larger unit and not in the artificially abstracted detail. We can know what certain insects are like, for instance, the fruitfly, without knowing much about their chromosomes or even their number. Returning to the larger question of truth in science, we know full well that much of the theorizing in science is not about what is perceptible to the eye. In setting up models, however, for verification, and in using the invisible for calculations, obviously a degree of uncertainty is introduced. The hypothesis can be discarded when it does not work, but when it does work it may, like subways, come above ground into the daylight and reveal a real truth about a perceptible object. This is what we all hope for in the immense labor undertaken to discover the causes of cancer.

In a book called *The Nature of Belief* I developed a view of "interpretation," as I called it, a mode of knowledge neither necessarily intuitive or inferential, whereby we could become quite certain that we were right. It differs from the kind of certainty to which Lord (Bertrand) Russell referred when he said that no one would take arsenic for breakfast on the ground that scientifically he could not be sure that it was poison. In other words, we know enough about nature to use the word "certainty" even though the necessity present be not of the logical or mathematical order. [6] But in many cases of interpretation there is no special scientific procedure. A good gamester represents what I mean on a level not strictly intellectual: the footballer, who is aware where his own side and where the opponents, where again the openings are and the distance he has to make before getting through. The good motorist is judging what to do with four or five problems at the same time, a child on the edge of the road, a wild driver behind him, a

[6] Once I was arguing with a young empiricist who resolutely rejected any kind of absolute certainty. I quoted to him a well-authenticated story of a man who had lost one leg being taken to a religious hospital. Next morning he had regained the lost leg. My adversary immediately said "Impossible" before he realized that he had denied his own position.

lorry approaching, and side roads drawing near. At cards some players have an uncanny sense both of the cards in the other man's hand and what he is going to play. We reach a higher level in interpreting abstruse texts and passages in a foreign language which we read with difficulty. What may be called sympathetic understanding is essential in reading verse or prose, seeing what Karl Rahner or Heidegger is trying to say and making sense of Rimbaud or a film like *Blow Up*. I have known philosophers with the most acute minds who would never read with sympathy the writings of other philosophers; they found "howlers" galore in the first few pages and ceased to read on. Language signs provide many instances of the kind of interpretation I mean, and in human intercourse it is constantly being used, in gestures of the hands, movements of the face and its expressions. We know when another person is sad or joyful, angry or pleased. Sympathy and love here heighten our perception and understanding. As a typical example take this: to the onlookers a baby being christened may look more like a monkey than a child of its parents, but the mother has seen the evidence already, the evidence that the child's face will be very like its father's. One other example which illustrates two forms of belief or certainty: a messenger comes with a letter saying that it is from an old friend. Here our belief rests on the word of the messenger, but on opening the letter the writing is so characteristic that we know immediately by whom it has been written.

Now in many instances we can be quite certain, and perhaps the most striking and least known is what an engineer named H. S. V. Bickford called "the Unity of Indirect Reference." He meant by this that we are constantly making remarks which rely for their truth on an indefinite number of facts that are rarely mentioned. If I tell X to look up some friends of mine when he goes to Paris, I make no reference to Paris being a city some distance away, with air or water to be traversed, and so forth. The number of items reaches to infinity, and when one of them does not fit the context we gradually feel something is wrong. An acquaintance, for instance, mentions Oxford and friends of mine he has met there. Very soon I wonder whether he is not mistaken, suspect he is fooling me or has never been to Oxford, until suddenly I realize he is talking about the town of Oxford near Memphis in Tennessee, where William Faulkner lived. In a mistake like this the whole world of communication can collapse, and we realize how ordinary remarks rest really on a concordance with an infinity of facts. This certainty then is thicker than any other of our certainties, guaranteed as it is by the consent of the universe we live in. It is this kind of knowledge which makes us not waste time looking up the evidence for the existence of Queen Victoria, or Cape Cod if I have never been there. Not that the certainty rests just upon the absence of discord, nor on our taking for granted a truth which so far as we know has never been contradicted. Bickford was referring to a capacity of the mind to recognize the kind of unity of evidence present when we say that Great Britain is an island, or that there is no invasion of England going on at this present moment. To quote from my *The Nature of Belief:*

If we may be allowed to speak of the external world making impressions on the mind, we can then picture the result as far more intricate than any work of bronze hammered by a Vulcan into a pattern. Every moment winged words strike us, sensations leave their effect, and in such a variety of ways as to cause bewilderment. Nevertheless, these hordes of impressions form into an order with a minute tracery like the facets of a fly's eye, nay, rather, a thousand spiders' webs worked into one pattern. Now when we recall that error consists in believing a thing to be what it is not and so believing something which is inconsistent with other facts, are we not forced to conclude that the absence of any such inconsistency in the myriad interlacing content of experience I have described is a mark of truth and a pledge of certainty? (pp. 198–9)

The late Merleau-Ponty seems to be saying something similar to this when he insists that we do not start life as solipsists, slowly coming to be sure that there is a real world around us and living persons in it. Our body takes charge of all that from the beginning, for our body is no more isolated from the physical world than our head is from our own body and nervous system. We are living in a physical world as a swimmer is aware that his medium is water; we articulate our experience by means of the body, which is the unperceived term in the center of the world; and toward it all objects turn their faces, for the world is seen from my bodily angle of vision. This view of Merleau-Ponty's is enlightening but I think that it needs supplementing, and demands a higher plateau from which we can form a very fair idea of what a true humanism should look like. He has told us how the body is a kind of pivot or lighthouse; but along with the body is the soul or spirit, which equally has its own world in which it is at home. It is the center and radar of the world of mind and spirit, and therefore from the first we are at home in a world where moral demands are made upon us and ideals flitter before our eyes. We know in our hearts that we must not fake, be content with half-measures, tolerate inaccuracy in our work as dentists, doctors, or scientists, that we must conserve our own independence and yet give of ourselves in personal relationships, which have to be pursued in a climate of justice, loyalty, and love. And as with the body the moon has been thought immemorially to affect not only the tides but the fevers of the brain, and the signs of the Zodiac and the heavenly bodies to influence the lives of individuals, so the presence—perhaps the living Presence—of beauty and goodness, as well as the ideal of truth, broods from on high over the spirit of man. These absolutes in their diversity endow the sensible order of reality with their special qualities, but never abrogate their sovereign power; the soul of man is at home in both worlds and can only advance by taking cognizance of both.

What is ever a matter for marveling is the interplay between these two worlds. Our sensible experience is all of a piece through the ministry of our bodies, and the same can be said about our intellectaal and spiritual experience because of the presence of the soul; but over and beyond this is the concordance, the power of symbols to give us entrance into a nonsensible order. What is beautiful to the senses has not only a spiritual equivalent but actually tells us of something new and real in the world of spirit, and in addition proves to be a good, whetting our appetites for still higher joys. When William Blake writes "Tyger! Tyger! burning bright/In the forests of the night," he has already transformed the animal prowling in the forests, so that we agree with his rhetorical question, "What immortal hand or eye/Dare frame thy fearful symmetry?" The "Countenance Divine" does "shine forth upon our clouded hills," and animal innocence intimates to us the meaning of holiness. To deny, therefore, certainties in life and absolutes is to abjure our humanity and shut out from our vision any fit ideal of humanism.

While pragmatic and positivist philosophies are in the ascendant there will be many in the academic field ready to deny certainties of any kind, and they may well point to the practice of the scientists. But in fact though scientists use techniques, models, and hypotheses which are always corrigible, they are not any the less dogmatic than the theologians of old. Witness Professor Medawar's scathing criticisms of both Teilhard de Chardin and Arthur Koestler, and Sir Julian Huxley's confidence in his own view of evolution and animadversions on those who disagree with him. Positive philosophers, also, seem to be moving away from their dogma that facts are always contingent and only such subjects as logic have to do with necessary propositions and certainty. Stuart Hampshire, for instance, writes in *Thought and Action* (Harper and Row, 1962) that "we must unavoidably think of reality as consisting of persisting things of different types and kinds"; and P. F. Strawson makes use of the expression "conceptual scheme" as conveniently describing "the frame of reality with which we have to work as human beings. There must be such a scheme which remains true despite all possible variations in place and time, culture and culture." "We think," he goes on, "of the world as containing particular things, some of which are independent of ourselves; we think of the world's history as made up of particular episodes in which we may or may not have a part, and we think of these particular things and events as included in the topics of our common discourse, as things about which we can talk to each other."

To use the language in vogue at the moment, Strawson is claiming that, whatever may be said about dynamic truths, static ones must be admitted if we are to give a proper account of the reality we experience. Now if such a "conceptual scheme" to describe "the frame of reality" is needed for our everyday discourse, we can well argue that a similar kind of permanent scheme is needed for our experience of the moral order, and even beauty has to submit to rules. *Securus judicat orbis terrarum.* The unanimous judgment, that is, of the simple and wise in every culture in admiring the truth and beauty, the earthly and transcendent appeal of a Queen Nefertiti, wife of Ikhnaton, or the elongated figures in the porch of Chartres, or the *Très Riches Heures* of Jean de Berry; not to mention what I hope will in time win all hearts, the static forms of Rouault, the magical inlay of Mary Bowling, and the many-windowed baptistery of David Jones's mind. In his *Abolition of Man*, C. S. Lewis brought together at the end of the book and under a heading called "Tao" many of the moral laws and sayings of Christian and Jewish teaching, the Koran and the code of Hammurabi, and the Hindu and Chinese saws and precepts. He thereby showed that mankind has relied on a common stock of morals, astonishingly the same despite the variations in time, place, culture, and tradition. This conformity in moral demands and ideas may have been in Heidegger's mind when he wrote that "there was another kind of knowledge besides the scientific to which science is subordinate, a fundamental existentialist form of knowing which gives a pattern for action and is understood by simple and learned alike."

This evidence demonstrates how permanent the basic structure of morality remains. The feelings are often relative to the situation and to new crises owing to famine or lack of water or racial rivalries and male and female domination—to mention only some of the causes. But normally emotions and knowledge, wishing and willing, settle happily together like birds in their sanctuary. This needs be said in order to rectify the modern impression that moral and other truths vary like the rules of different games. Humanism should not be regarded as a chameleon, nor truth as a kind of ectoplasm coming from heaven knows where and vanishing without reason. There is all the difference between standards which belong to human nature and yet suffer from maltreatment and misunderstanding and a Caliban-Ariel being who is neither man, fowl, fish, nor good red herring. Variation within unity is explicable; variation without unity is unintelligible. It is the former which is permanent in history. The intellect can be duped by the passions and an overheated imagination, for reason, as Aristotle said truly, moves nothing of itself and so needs an interest, a motive, to spark it.[7]

One other caveat: the contemporary dislike of immobile truths is not to be judged as wholly wrongheaded. To regard truths as stones dropped from the sky is almost as ill-judged as to regard truth as in every way a wager and

[7] A Christian friend of mine told me how he had a severe bout of melancholia, and during it he never stirred because he had lost all interest in religion, in family, friends, and work. But when I asked him had he lost his religious faith, he replied, "Certainly not!" He believed it to be true while he had lost all inclination to practice it.

chancy. Perfection surely lies between the two extremes. History is not a record of static, unchanging ideas. So perverse a view led Benedetto Croce and R. G. Collingwood to press for an equally extreme view, namely, that the past lives only in the present. The dead is ever coming to life in the present judgment. More temperate is the view of some of the writers already mentioned who harp on the dynamic character of truth. Inevitably they tend to contrast words like "dynamic" and "static," relegating the latter to unhistorical habits of though in past ages. Valuable as their strictures on past thinkers may be, they nevertheless leave us with a problem—the problem which is expressed in the very word "evolution." The question is not that a truth changes completely nor that it remains unchanged. What all of us want to know is how a doctrine, for example, can be permanent and nevertheless grow: how, without losing its static virtue, it can acquire a dynamic quality. The learned today have run off to worship at the shrine of the god of probability, which means the apotheosis of betting. What corresponds with this in the arts is the Jazzfest. Better surely to have one certain Providence, one true God, ever the same, who allows us to know more and more about Him, our friends, nature, and ourselves.

prove it by cooking. What a long education in time was needed, with many disasters until the rules were established which would be handed on and bettered!

We forget all this in our longstanding civilization, and take for granted innumerable lessons painfully learned, customs and laws which save our society from slipping back into chaos. We naturally are preoccupied with what is yet to be, and so much of our lives is taken for granted and unnoticed. Steadily we work to get better physical and moral conditions and settlements between citizen and citizen, class and class, state and state. For the rest we accept sidewalks and houses, clothes and trains, all the things comprised under Marx's definition of freedom, the necessities we are conscious of. Inadequate as this definition is when applied to human relations where real freedom is operative, it summarizes and tallies with our knowledge and acceptance of the laws of chemistry and physics and electricity. It is in this structured society, which rests on innumerable truths experienced and scientifically determined, that our fully human activities can operate. Laws are made and customs cherished, and gradually with the steadily growing appreciation of liberty and liberties the sanctity of human life becomes an accepted principle. The English common law, for instance, provides that an individual is to be judged innocent until he is proved guilty; and it assigns rights to all human persons be they men, women, children, colored or sick or imbecile. Hereby freedom sets up its own splendid absolutes; and as in law, so in medicine. The Hippocratic Oath dates back probably to the fourth century B.C. and it has words which the young doctor has to repeat, words such as these: "That you will exercise your art solely for the care of your patients, and will give no drug, perform no operation, for a criminal purpose." Within the state, too, and within groups inside each state, there are established codes based on immemorial laws, rules, for example, of courtesy, behavior with the other sex at table, extending to the treatment of strangers, and most exactly at court and in chapel.

At one time privilege was intended to rest on the performance of high duties, and it was a happy thought which led to the giving of a central place in Westminster Abbey to the tomb of the Unknown Warrior. In this act one of the most profound of human emotions found expression. Humanism without a capital letter shows its features more and more clearly as time goes on, and embodies itself in codes and laws which bring out men's regard for each other, for knowledge, virtue, and God. If then a being from another planet were to visit the earth, he would be impressed by the genius of man in controlling this world and creating out of it so much that ministers to his needs and desires. He would learn of the improvement in the conditions of life, of the factories turning out goods serving man's needs, of the marvelous means of transportation, and the provision for amusement, learning, and leisure. But he would miss the special quality which makes the beings of this earth human if he were not introduced into the moral and mystical worlds of Japan and China, the abiding search for bliss and unity in Hindu and Buddhist philosophy. He would come to see that man has always built his cities with a central spot, an omphalos symbolizing the meeting place of heaven and earth. Then Jerusalem and Mecca and Rome would mean more to him than any grandiose tower, even the highest of skyscrapers. Conducted now by his own desire through Sancta Sophia, San Zeno and Chartres and King's College Chapel and other cloisters and beauties, he would be in no doubt that humanism was not self-enclosed but had a vision of a love which was beyond its conceiving, a meeting of human and divine agapé.

The conclusion, therefore, of one who looks back at history is that no humanism could be complete which left out religion. This in past ages would usually be accepted, but now it has become a matter of debate. Man has changed from being a child and has become a self-sufficient grown-up. I have said that in the past the skeptics would have been in a small minority. Prometheus is their champion, but in the myth he has to live chained to a rock and suffering torments. In former times in his struggle for existence man felt the odds were so strong against him that he must seek aid from the power behind or in or above nature. Nature, like the sea, could be at one moment a friend and the next a terrifying hostile power. Hence the image of the faun, now smiling, childlike and propitious, and also lascivious as a satyr and malicious. Ignorant of the workings of his own body as well as of the natural world around him, man suffered bad accidents continually, and he was hardly better off in the company of his fellow men. Every day meant a possible mishap, a sting, bite, or fall, or damaging storm or flood. Every journey was perilous, and at home a contagious disease or a drought or famine could kill him and his family or turn him into a vagabond. Many died at childbirth, and only the strong could be reared; even their span of life was short. No wonder that the forces around men seemed alive with personalities benign or destructive, to be prayed to or propitiated. Karl Marx was not prejudiced in holding that primitive and feudal man was in many ways so helpless that he needed the comfort of assistance from a benevolent deity. Religion could serve as a sop: but it was a mistake on his part and an insult to human nature to restrict religion to this one function. The motto *Per ardua ad astra* shows us better the mettle of man. Thomas More, as good a humanist as England ever produced, could say in a dark squalid dungeon of the Tower of London, "God maketh a wanton of me and fondleth and dangleth me more in Tower." As against Marx it is remarkable that even when the ideas of an afterlife were dim and the gods were mostly silent, nevertheless religion, far from fading out, flourished the more. It would be nearer the truth to say that religion—meaning by it a sense of dependence on God and an aspiration to be drawn into the divine perfection and loveliness—must be deeply inset in man's consciousness. Even fate, which at first looks as if it treated human beings as pawns, could be transformed into a providential destiny, as in the lines spoken when leaving the isle of Lemnos by Philoctetes in Sophocles' play: "Farewell, O plain of Lemnos, girt by the sea, and send me forth blameless and with good intent: thither where great Fate and the good will of friends are bringing me, and the Lord, Master of all, who has ordained this to happen."

The Israelites in their early history, as it is generally held —though the Ugaritic texts may well modify this view— took for granted that man had only one life to live and that on this earth. Nevertheless, throughout their literature there is the sense of a saving God who can not only deliver them from all foes, but make them noble in mind, wise and kind-hearted, holy, in fact, as their God was holy and without flaw.

This sense of God and understanding of His ways made for an alliance in former days between religion and humanism. So close was this alliance, as I have said, at times the two could not be taken apart. The Buddha no doubt according to tradition was stirred by the misery of the lives lived around him and taught a way of life which would remove all anxiety and phenomenal self-consciousness; but what he taught was not purely negative, as is proved by the influence of his teaching on the civilization of India, China, and Japan. In the West, Neoplatonism demanded of its adherents a flight from the fascinations of the temporal, but still kept one foot on earth, for as Plotinus wrote: "The flight we read of consists not in quitting earth, but in living our earth life with justice and piety in the light of philosophy." Not only Neoplatonism contradicts Marx concerning the reason for belief in religion or the spiritual life. The Stoics also thought that a withdrawal from the world was necessary, but this could be done while engaged in mundane affairs. Seneca was a busy man, but maintained that he was fulfilling the Stoic ideal if in the midst of noise he could be at peace and in quiet within himself: and Marcus Aurelius argued that there was no need to run away from day-to-day life. That would be "very unlike a philosopher," for a philosopher "may at any hour retreat within" himself. He obviously from his own practice believed that the philosopher, and this kind of a philosopher, could combine ruler and priest in one. Indeed already here is adumbrated an answer to the question which will have to be taken up later, whether there can and should be a humanism allied to religion.

The Christian religion is called a supernatural one, and therefore its relation to humanism needs special treatment. Light can be thrown on this subject by looking at the story of Christianity. Having a special status as a historical religion, some of its advocates are of opinion that this smooths the way to a working agreement with the secular city. But this perhaps is to make too much of the Christian Church's historicity. In the Gospels, Christ does not train his disciples to play an active part in cities or societies. He keeps quietly aloof from the burning questions of the day to Jews, namely, how to free themselves from Roman domination and regain their ancient glories. When presented with Caesar's coin, he breaks in two the problem by which his enemies hoped to embarrass him; and when Pilate asks him directly where he stands in national matters, he answers that his kingdom is not of this world. Clearly, therefore, there is some ambiguity here; God became man as Christianity teaches, and Christianity itself is a historical visible body, looking beyond this world in its teaching and aims. For centuries this problem could be shelved, for at first the majority, if not all, Christians were expecting a speedy return of Christ and the end of time. This kept them from being too immersed in the life around them. Then again Christians were given little chance to participate in the civilization of Rome. They were persecuted and had to hide, and this no doubt developed a habit of mind. The morals, too, of the first centuries in Rome and elsewhere provided easy material for the bishops in their homilies. They could but warn their flocks of the vices rampant, the brutalities of the theater and colosseum, the unnatural sex relations, the corruption and disgusting religious practices of which we read in Tacitus and Suetonius, Juvenal and Petronius and other writers. St. Augustine's *City of God*, with its famous distinction between the two cities, must be read in the light of this. He saw around him little evidence that the City of Man could so improve as to cooperate with the City of God.

When, however, the Roman Empire had been undone by the barbarian invasions, new ideas were in the air. At first the barbarians looked even less attractive than the pagan Romans; after all Rome had established a civilized world of law, and the Neoplatonic and Stoic philosophies and poets like Vergil had created and sustained a high level of culture. But the barbarians were easier to convert, and when converted they roused the idea, the dream maybe, of a Christian civilization, a graced humanity. Education fell into the hands of Christian clerics, and Charlemagne sent for scholars from Ireland, England, and France to form a school of learning, which in time blossomed into what have come to be known as universities. Such universities as Padua and Bologna, Paris and Oxford, were the first fruits of the liaison of the Church with the world. A premature Christian humanism came into being when, as Christopher Dawson has pointed out, the papacy took under its protection the Cluniacs and Cistercians of the North, and the Church served as the ultimate bond of unity. There were social antagonisms, "as strong as they are today, but they were antagonisms within a common society." As William Langland writes, "He called that house Unity—which is Holy Church in English." Monks and friars led or preached crusades, and St. Bernard was the counselor of kings as well. The habit of making priests Lord Chancellors continued to the time of Wolsey in England and later in France. All students at Oxford and Cambridge were tonsured clerks. So it was that the Christian view of life, even though it might not be put into practice, penetrated every town, street, and corner. Artists chose or were given without questioning Christian subjects to paint or carve, whether the patrons were popes or kings, bishops, princes, or nobles. The rough manners and tastes of the North were refined by contact with Near-Eastern and Moorish cultures. By the eleventh century the military owner of land was inducted into an order of chivalry, thus making the fighting man gentle and chivalrous to women. The theory was always far ahead of the practice at a time when barbarism still stayed beneath the varnish. It meant, however, instead of the confusion of inequality today, due to differences of wealth, an order of degrees based on service to God and fellow men. It is commended in the speech of Ulysses in Shakespeare's *Troilus and Cressida:*

> How could communities,
> Degrees in schools and brotherhoods in cities,
> Peaceful commerce from dividable shores,
> The primogeniture and due of birth,
> Prerogative of age, crowns, sceptres, laurels,
> But by degree stand in authentic place?
> Take but degree away, untune that string,
> And hark what discord follows!

The result is "to make a sop of all this solid globe." Here Shakespeare is presenting what was evidently the outlook of the humanist of the Middle Ages. The life of man living in a state of nature, to quote an author born long after the medieval order had broken down, Thomas Hobbes, was "solitary, poor, nasty, brutish and short." The medieval cleric and statesman believed that in this state of nature man, like the jungle, ran wild without the discipline imposed by the ideals man could and should live for. R. W. Southern quotes in his lecture on *Scientific Humanism* the lines of a medieval schoolmaster:

> The animals express their brute creation
> By head hung low and downward looking eyes.
> But man holds high his head in contemplation
> To show his natural kinship with the skies.

This hopeful view of human nature was essentially a Christian one. At the advent of Christianity the mood in the Greco-Roman world was one of melancholy, if not despair. That outstanding Englishman of the twelfth century, once chancellor of Oxford University, Robert Grosseteste, assigns the reason for the change to belief in the high destiny of mortal man. Writing in 1230 he set down his Franciscan view of Creation and Redemption, one which gave more glory to man even than St. Thomas Aquinas. "The Incarnation would have happened even if man had never sinned; it was necessary to complete man's natural glory. Since human nature is capable of union with God, God must from the beginning have intended to crown man's natural endowments by sharing his nature. In this act the natural creation was completed: man became the keystone of the whole natural order which found its consolidating principle in him." This is a far cry from Marx's idea of religion: it might better serve as a motto and inspiration to the astronauts moving out to meet the stars and the far spaces.

It is in keeping with the exalted view of man and of the power of the spirit and God's grace that coronations and degree-taking at universities followed rites akin to that of the ordination of priests. All offices were hedged about with divinity, and all civil and academic works had a religious side to them and touched on mystery. Examples are to be seen in what we now call trade unions but in the Middle Ages were known as guilds and livery companies. They had rules controlling competition, demanding fair work, and it was their duty and honor to serve the community. They met in church and proceeded under the patronage of a saint, St. Crispin, for instance. Medicine also was seen in the image of the Good Samaritan of the Gospels, and St. Luke, evangelist and physician. As a result came the novel institution of hospitals and hospitaller knights. Law provides another outstanding example of this too short-lived humanism; the common law, which now is in force in nearly the whole of the English-speaking world, was an invention of the Middle Ages. The makers of it were English priests, Bracton, Fortescue, and others. Of their work Pollock and Maitland have this to say: "Those few men who were gathered at Westminster round Pateshall and Raleigh and Bracton were penning writs that would run in the name of kingless commonwealths on the other shore of the Atlantic ocean. They were making right and wrong for us and for our children." Through them the ideal of the free and lawful man (*liber et legalis homo*) was then brought down to earth at a time when old pagan customs still persisted, the lowly position of women, for example, and the petty servitude of the serf. This common law Vinogradoff declared to be "the necessary outcome of the conviction that the world was created and is governed by divine providence."

> For we are all
> Christ's creatures. And of his coffers rich
> And brethren of one blood: alike beggars and earls.

This attempt to develop a Christian humanism did not last. It rested on a belief that there was a supernatural order, the order of grace, and a natural order. By "supernatural" was meant the special gift given in Christ that in him and through him and with him mere human beings could be raised to a new relationship with God. By this relationship men could become co-heirs with Christ, sons of God in the sense in which Christ himself was the Son of God. In short, man could be divinized, the while preserving his human personality. By the natural order was understood all that man is capable of doing, thinking, and being by his own powers.[1] The hope expressed in the cooperation of Church and State, City of God and City of Man, was never fully realized, but it made a priceless contribution not only in art and church building and law, but in a tradition of behavior and personal self-regard. I have already quoted the lines, "We are all Christ's creatures." Even the simplest peasant had learned this, and with it had developed a sense of freedom and personal rights—long before the Renaissance. He was protected by the common law, and in the Church in the sight of God he knew himself to be the equal of peers, princes, and popes. Such a knowledge led on to the later realization embodied in the cry for Liberty, Equality, and Fraternity. There is no inherent reason why man by his natural capacity should not arrive at these truths, but the fact is that the ideal of free men under God came to life in the West and spread from there to other parts of the world. The codes of other civilizations embraced moral truths, but what was wanting in them was a clear impression of personal identity and worth. It may be that the temptations of the few to power were too strong, as Popper seems to suggest, and the populace, because of food shortage and climate, were too lethargic. The sad fact stands out that far too often unfortunately in every land man has been his own worst enemy, *Homo homini lupus.*

Be that as it may, the experiment of the Middle Ages failed. There have been many various causes assigned for

[1] This meaning of the natural order is important as bearing on the modern secular views of, for example, Harvey Cox, the author of *The Secular City.*

this: minor ones, such as the plague which decimated Europe and the disaster of the Hundred Years' War; major ones, such as the growth of freedom itself and nationhood and the corruption of the Church. The unity achieved by the Church was won at a price. It meant that there was only one truth and one way of life, and what opposed ought to be put down or exterminated. Even the wisest of ecclesiastical rulers perhaps could not have ensured a unified flourishing international society so dependent on Church teaching and discipline. As it happened, many of the rulers fell far below the standards required of them. A Marxist would interpret all this in terms of dialectical materialism as the changeover of a feudal society to a capitalist one. The less prejudiced historians point to the growth of nationalism, the discovery of new worlds, and, above all, to the new and independent scientific spirit, which is both symbolized and realized in the story of Galileo.

What now all would agree on is that if a Christian humanism is once more attempted it must vary considerably from that of the Middle Ages. More pointedly we have to ask whether such an ideal is any longer even a possibility. The Church may have an answer, and that remains to be seen; but what its attitude has been since the Renaissance and Reformation until the Second Vatican Council we know. Long before the Council of Trent those concerned for the well-being of the Catholic Church begged for reforms. The condition of the Church was lamentable—with many abuses, widespread corruption, an illiterate clergy, and a scandalous papal court and papacy. The Council of Trent took steps to set matters right, and as far as can be judged it laid the blame for the rampant evils on the clergy being more interested in the world than in the things of God. The City of Man had defiled the City of God, and instead of priests and leaders of the Church acting as a salt to keep the world fresh, the salt had lost its savor; the spiritual had succumbed to the secular. The lesson to be learned was one which the early Church had put into practice: "Seek ye first the kingdom of God and all things shall be added to you." Put first things first, the everlasting before the temporal, the kingdom of God before all human ambitions. This was not a declaration of the complete separation on principle of the two powers, but it assumed that the Gospel command of self-denial, penance and abstinence, prayer and mortification, was to be taken seriously and as part of the sanctification of the soul. The discipline of the Church was tightened, religious life apart from any secular pursuits encouraged, methods of asceticism and contemplation were taught, and heroic virtue held up as the ideal needed for success in converting the world. This policy was successful in ·that it got rid of much of the corruption and produced a remarkable galaxy of saints and missionary martyrs; but it meant that the Church dropped behind in the race for new knowledge and turned into an absentee, watching what was going on around it but not participating. The next three hundred years can be called a period of reform, of what Maritain has called spiritual athleticism, a long long Lent during which the Church built up its strength as generation after generation of clerics and good layfolk went through individually the exercises of the spiritual life. The texts in the New Testament which dealt with abnegation and the image of Christ crucified dominated the new churches; so much so, indeed, that many came to emphasize the transitoriness of the world and regard all action as a waste product unless done from a supernatural motive. It is not surprising, then, that many tended to regard any concern for secular things as not only dangerous but foolish—a devilish piece of nonsense. A line such as Aubrey de Vere's could serve as a text in any pulpit, "Love thy God and love Him only and thy heart shall be secure."

Such a view was bound to make the life of a man living in the world very difficult, for he had somehow to reconcile what seemed to be in opposition, namely, a life for God alone, and a life with love and duties toward family and natural interests in work and play. Attempts to solve the problem occurred sporadically, and they have increased considerably within the last few decades. One of the reasons why Teilhard de Chardin has been received with such acclaim is probably because of the nature of his answer to this problem. It also heralded the beginning of new, because forgotten, attitudes of the Church to modern society and its problems and ideals. The long Lent looks to be over, and the Church has entered the lists not to fight the good secularist but to work side by side with him in the regeneration of society.

The problem of a Christian humanism, if there can be such a form of life, I have said, is changed. There is no longer a unified Christendom. With the rise of the Reformed Churches went the breakup of a unified society into national states with the active principle of *Cujus regio ejus religio*. The assumption by Henry VIII of the headship of the Church in England was important at the time, and has resulted in a national Church with all the inconveniences of Parliament being able to dictate forms of religious prayer and observance and to appoint to bishoprics. Nevertheless it managed to keep much of its freedom, more so than in some other states where it became almost completely subservient to the ruling power. A more formidable difficulty in the way of any real *rapprochement* of Christianity with secular society is the change of culture from one of the liberal arts to that of science and technology. By the seventeenth century secular learning and the empirical outlook already challenged Church domination and theological doctrines. This movement toward a secularist society was accelerated as the Church had less to say that was relevant, and science took a hold upon man's imagination and interests by its startling discoveries and the gigantic strides made in improving the conditions of life. When bishop and scientist met in battle during the nineteenth century, there came no agreement, only the defeat of the cleric and the worsening of his prestige in public opinion. To some the contest between Church and State, supernatural religion and secularism, seems now to be over. Secularism has won hands down. To the rationalist this spells the gradual extinction of religion, with only one philosophy of life, and only one world in which man can work out his destiny. To some Christians, however, it means a *volte face* but not the end of Christianity. This view has been taken up in many quarters ever since the posthumous letters of Dietrich Bonhoeffer were published, and his views with those of Bultmann and Tillich popularized by Bishop J. A. Robinson in *Honest to God*.

The rationalists form a heterogeneous company. We have seen something of them already. They include Lord (Bertrand) Russell and philosophers like Professor A. J. Ayer and Professor Lamont of Columbia University, and, I suppose, Sir Julian Huxley. Russell in his autobiography, to set off his anticlerical bias, shows a passionate interest in religion, especially in its mystical forms, and Huxley makes almost a religion of his evolution, conferring on it many religious attributes which might stir awe and reverence if not worship! I have already quoted from Kathleen Nott, one of those who are wholeheartedly in favor of the shapes human life is taking and ask for nothing better. Less positive are those who look at the modern scene and judge that religion as the dominant factor in past civilizations is yielding place to physical science or the social sciences. Lord Annan, for example, in his Romanes Lecture in 1965, spoke of this change in the frame of mind of the educated man. In former times it was, as he said, the humanist cleric who had a monopoly in learning, Chaucer's Clerk of Oxenford or Wyclif or William of Wykeham. But now it is "the social sciences which are thought to be the key to learning." What corresponds to the sage of ancient times is now the famous scientist, who is given a Nobel prize. H. J. Brabham, in his *Religion in Modern Society,* would like to see the Churches recognize that they have become a small minority in the nation. Hence they ought to give up their privileged position and try to live in freedom, of course, but modestly, as befits the insignificant group they have become. Such an opinion may be in keeping with the lack of interest in religion amongst the working classes of the industrialized nations and the movement toward a form of senate composed of those who stand out as highly skilled in a managerial society.

It is easy—and too commonly done—to put humanists and agnostics and atheists together, or at least as converging toward one another. But it is quite possible for an atheist not only to disbelieve in God but also in his fellow men. The early cynics were not conspicuous for their love of mankind, and Schopenhauer and Thomas Hardy in *The Dynasts* looked on human life as a sorry jest. Humanism, if it is taken to mean a belief in human nature to such a degree that man is held to be capable of creating a perfect life out of his own resources, ignores God and religion, and is therefore agnostic by disposition. On the other hand, if we mean by humanism merely that men and women should develop their own powers and rely upon them so far as possible, then it is compatible with religion. Indeed, it was a religious genius who said, "Pray to God as if all depended upon him, and act as if all depended on yourself." It was in defense of the first kind of humanist that Lord Willis and Lord Francis-Williams spoke on television. The one said that humanism was a faith by which it is possible to live. Man could live on moral principles without the help of a God. The answer to life lay in man's own hands, and his purpose should be to try by his own efforts to change the world. Lord Francis-Williams said very much the same thing, but made this special point, so typical of the modern mind, that all the intellectual efforts to explain or understand the world were barren. The philosophers would do well to teach us how to live; they do no good to themselves or anybody else when they lose themselves in metaphysics or religious speculation. We know enough for practical living, and we should be content with that.

This shows a rather surprising confidence in the ability of the nonreligious moralists to show us the way of life. They generally fight very shy of giving us advice: in fact many of them have no advice to give. As we have seen, Miss Kathleen Nott and Kingsley Martin are frank about this, and confess that they know of no simple or soft answers. A. J. Ayer finds it difficult from the philosophical position he has taken up to give even a semirational account of morals. More recently (*Encounter,* June 1966) he has admitted that in one sense humanism is a harsh doctrine.

To insist that life has only the meaning that one succeeds in giving it; that we have only this short amount of time to experience any happiness or accomplish anything of value is all very well for people who are living in easy circumstances and have been given the opportunity to develop intellectual and cultural interests. For those who are ignorant, helpless and in material want, it is small consolation only that their miseries will end with death, and throughout history the majority of human beings have been in this condition. It would therefore be insensitive, if not hypocritical, for humanists to preach their doctrines unless they believed that the values which they set on human experience and achievement were capable of being realised not merely by a privileged minority but by mankind in general. Even if they cannot be assured that this will ever be so, they at least have the moral obligation to do what they can to make it possible.

This, so to call it, apologia is, as most would admit, both moving and high-minded in its frankness and intentions and hopes. It is nevertheless a curiously revealing document. Professor Ayer has passed through many phases since he wrote *Language, Truth and Logic,* but his main empirical line of thought has on the whole been consistently the same. Now when he first wrote, he considered moral and religious experiences to be no more than "emotional noises," and though he would now pay moral experience much more respect, I do not think he has yet come to accept it as a form of experience which can be called rational, that is, open to being called true or false. As a result he is still, like Lord (Bertrand) Russell, hard put to it to find justification for his most creditable moral sentiments. Both he and Russell can be passionate in their indignation at cruelty and injustice. On their own philosophical premises this indignation is a private feeling and no more. We all have private feelings, and they are our own concern, and we have to accept the situation, which is like that of Jack Sprat and his wife, where one could not bear fat and the other could not eat lean meat. They could not reasonably say to one another you must detest lean because I detest it. How then can Ayer write as if humanists could and should go beyond these private feelings to make others agree with them? Ayer in his last sentence writes of a "moral obligation" to do what we can to make others happy. One can never get a moral obligation out of a private feeling, any more than a man whose nerves become upset by the singing of birds can morally assume that the whole neighborhood has the same dislike or ought to have it. There is no room, so far as I can see, for "moral obligation" in much modern philosophy, at any rate in the traditional sense in which the words are used. Furthermore, we can well ask what is meant in the humanist manifesto by "happiness," the happiness which all persons without any limitation are capable of enjoying. It is our duty to strive to work for this. But is it, whatever it consists in, more than a dream? Is it a practical possibility? Doubt is bound to rise in the mind when Ayer admits that the majority of the human race has never had this happiness, and that the generation he is addressing is also fairly sure not to enjoy it. This generation must live without hope of winning it, and rest on a hope that generations to come may have a better fate. With the nature of happiness left so vague, and the possibility of it also denied to so many, Ayer's state of felicity looks more like a horizon than a reality, and we will have to absent ourselves from it for a very long time.

What is also a little disconcerting is that even if some of the obstacles standing in the way of happiness were removed, I do not see that we would be much nearer to perfect bliss. Governments, and individuals as well, are now greatly concerned to remove obstacles in the way of a proper human life. The fight is continuous against disease and the causes of disease; pain may in not too far off a time be eliminated, and so too crippling poverty and ugly surroundings and stunted education. But he would be a bold man who claimed that with the removal of these obstacles we should be within sight of a general and individual happiness. I fear that what is more likely is that the human race would die for lack of stimulus. Biologically the organs and muscles of the body degenerate when they have nothing to resist. And even supposing that all physical shortcomings are removed, it is surely true that the main source of trouble is still there; for it is out of the heart that comes the evil which pollutes or is obnoxious. I see a figure bending and writing with his finger on the ground, and the so-called righteous stepping away as he asks, "Who amongst you is without sin?" It is the skid rows and the Dachaus and Berchtesgadens of the mind which are the real obstacles in the way of the humanist ideal. (As I write I see a review of *The Trial of Ezra Pound*. When he was a child who could have thought that his life would be so checkered and that he would himself help to make it a purgatory?) Those who are computer-mad foresee a very different world from that of Ayer, one which is like a nightmare to Professor Louis Sohn, a Harvard lawyer. In a report for the Commission to Study the Organization for Peace, he says that all power will pass into "the hands who feed the data to the computers on which decisions are based and who are the interpret-

ers and implementers of the answers given by the computers. . . . If all the available data are integrated and stored
in a computer in a way permitting instantaneous access to
the record of each person, a sword of Damocles is going to
hang all the time over the head of everybody. . . . We
shall be able with computers and electronic devices to pre-
dict prenatally a child's physical characteristics and manipulate them to change the future of the human race" to accord with the preconceptions of those who are in control.
Altogether it seems many humanists are not sufficiently
realistic in their thinking! Nearer to the truth about man's
legitimate expectations are surely these lines:

> When one's friends hate each other
> How can there be peace in the world?
> Their asperities diverted me in my green time
> A blown husk that is finished
> But the light sings eternal
> A pale flare over marshes
> Where the salt hay whispers to tide's change
> Time   Space
> Neither life nor death is the answer.

While quoting I am reminded of an amusing letter to
Time magazine (October 14, 1966), which may have made
many think again on the possibility of saving the world by
economics and surgical skills, by drugs or on a psychiatrist's
couch. "Your essay," it reads ("Popping the Psyche"), "reveals the subconscious, repressed, latent, homosexual,
anxiety-ridden, amateur psychologist's traumatic depend-
ency on the compulsive, depressing gullibility of the con-
fused, simple, inferiority-complex, suffering American
public." This is far too hard on the patient psychiatrists,
but the pessimism in it, though exaggerated, is widespread.
How easy it would be to quote from leading dramatists and
novelists passages which illustrate the current pessimistic
mood and a fear that life is meaningless. Others harp upon

the growing anonymity as by mass communication millions of minds are "swamped with deluges of imprecision." There "lurks," as J. H. Plumb says, "a Salteena-like *alter ego* who wakes up at night from a nightmare of being fed into a cyclotron by Lord Snow and Professor Fred Hoyle."

There is naturally another side to the picture. Most men and women do seem to derive contentment out of life as it is, and this may well be the strongest argument in favor of a secular humanism, if we grant also that the conveniences of living will go on steadily increasing. The comforting fact, borne out by experience and history, is that man has an astonishing capacity of adapting himself to whatever form of life he finds or has imposed upon him. Supposedly educated members of a Chinese embassy reading the words of Mao as if they are of divine origin; Arabs with their feet in a cloaca and their eyes fixed on the skies. Apathy, no doubt, plays a part, and the soul hibernates. When, however, there is purpose and the endurance has a meaning, the mud and cold of trench life and even the horrors of a concentration camp can become bearable. We know too little of much of the past to be sure of its evidence, but a case can be argued that the natives of Africa in more primitive days, the Gypsies who wandered in their insanitary caravans from place to place, the peasant in Anatolia or Calabria, the poor—the multitudes of those who have lived in the fields and the ghetto and the slums—may for all we know have been as happy as many of the workers now in the great industrial cities. Such a judgment may seem absurd—more so to those who have had experience of the horrible diseases, such as leprosy, to which the more primitive peoples are liable, the diseases which Albert Schweitzer did so much in his hospital at Lambarene to check and heal. Nevertheless those who have worked in slums will testify to the neighborliness of the poor, their interest in family details and joy in little things. We feel in our bones, of course, that the victims of the factory system in former days, when the poor lived without drains or healthy food or proper doctoring, could not possibly be as contented as a modern working man. One is bound to give a qualified assent to this; all the same, suffering and privations here, as in war, created comradeship and affection which are hard to replace. It is the old story: riches can make the heart sad and comfort breeds selfishness.

Few of us realize how much our enjoyments are related to our expectations. How disappointed we are when our expectations have been roused by the hope that we have won a scholarship, are to receive a handsome present, or be given a holiday or a raise in pay, and then they fail to be fulfilled. Those who expect little and are constantly taken by surprise as they proceed through the years enjoy life the most. They are the last to grumble or resent their lot. Their attitude is one long thanksgiving. We nowadays know too much and have in some ways been spoilt, like children who have presents poured upon them. The more civilized we become and the better the conditions, the more do we expect. Our ancestors did not grow angry because walking or riding took more time than traveling by train or in the air. Even within living memory notes had to be carried around because there was no telephone. The rich who made the grand tour in the eighteenth and early nineteenth century were content if at the hotels hot water was brought in by cans and bathtubs provided. Such hotel conditions would not be tolerated now by the ordinary citizen on holiday. Hence the ninth beatitude: Blessed are they who do not expect, for they shall not be disappointed. I said above that where hardship has a meaning or is endured with a purpose it can heighten pleasure instead of diminishing it. Those two who chose to row the Altantic, the men and women who swim the English Channel, the Marco Polos and Cooks, the Livingstones and the Lawrences, continue the tradition of the St. Michaels and the St. Georges, for where there are no external dangers to overcome there are still commitments which involve danger and death, and joy is drawn out of these. Resistances, it cannot be repeated too often, are needed as a fillip or spice to action. They are as meat and drink to the hero of mythology. Nature tells the same tale, for the resistance of the air is necessary for the swallow and the skylark, and only by exercise can the muscles and organs of the body keep healthy. Fanatics may overdo it, but we are told that St. Simeon Stylites on his high pillar prayed, ate, and slept in great contentment.

Humanism, therefore, cannot be soft, and if it is to be hard does it not need the stimulus of religion and the example of the ascetics? These ascetics show the power of the human spirit to overcome bodily needs and ingrained habits. Apollo in his perfect symmetry, is he not to be outclassed by the elongated figures in the niches and on the portals of Chartres Cathedral? Fanatics in the Far East can go without food or sleep for incredible lengths of time. I do not say they should be imitated, but they make their limbs and bodies as flexible and docile as a piece of elastic; they walk over red-hot embers and swallow fire and snakes. Less startling, and perhaps more edifying as showing a respect for the human body, are some of the practices of the Christian saints. They have, nevertheless, followed a course of life very different from that usually advocated by humanists. (The distinguished lecturer and writer on moral philosophy, the Reverend Rashdall Hastings, once complained that St. Francis of Assisi had not been "respectable.") All of these saints, following the Sermon on the Mount, chose poverty and lives of heroic self-denial; they rejected what most would deem the world's best prizes, success, honor as well as money; they gave themselves completely to the service of God and their neighbors. To be rid of self-love they practiced austerities which are frightening, and yet their diaries and the verdicts of those who lived with them make clear that they possessed an inner peace and joy which stirred all to admiration. If this had been true of only one or two, judgment on them would necessarily be uncertain; but there is a long record of men and women of different ages of life and of different races who exhibit this serenity and joy, apostles, missionaries, great thinkers like Augustine and Bonaventure, founders of hospitals, nurses of the sick and plague-stricken, mystics like Teresa of Avila, and teachers and trainers of youth like Don Bosco. I do not think that the secular humanists have paid enough attention to this variation within human nature. It is as if a writer were to give, as he thought, an exhaustive enumeration of the different kinds of bears and left out the polar one.

In answer, the secularist might say that my examples are taken from the past, and it is with the present and future that we have to deal. Now modern men and women have already decided the matter. There is no doubt about a growing indifference to religion. The churches, we are told, are emptying and prayer is already a relic of the past. As advertisements have shown beyond all question, a product must appeal to some human need or desire if it is going to sell, and the truth is, we are told, that religion has lost its appeal. Modern man feels no need for it. This, I think, is a slippery argument. Children do not like taking medicine, "the whining school-boy with his satchel" creeps "like snail unwillingly to school," a fair percentage of women dislike mathematics, writers of poetry have a relatively small number of readers, and, sad to relate, publishers, if they keep to only the most intellectual and noble kinds of books, soon go out of business. An older type of apologist would retort that the disastrous results of the neglect of religion are already showing themselves in the growing lawlessness of youth, the increase of suicides, and the general lowering of standards in respect both of the unborn and the born.

We may, however, admit that there would be some force in this argument were democracy and humanism clearly producing a pattern of life which outstripped the Christian one in its splendor and finality. Few would claim that this was happening, and here again one can appeal to the evidence of the type of prisoners in law courts, the harsh unsentimentality of the modern novel, and the racial and social unrest. Only a materialist—and by that I mean one who views man as no more than a high-conditioned animal —could look with satisfaction at the objects which now attract both young and old. It is not that the young are ceasing to go to church because they have found a more sublime alternative to that offered in the Christian teaching. Views of life such as Christianity or Marxism, which require some mental effort or discipline, are brushed aside in the presence of immediate attractions, pop music and dance, dating, the movies and television, and games of all kinds. Dr. Leary can set himself up as a prophet to the young by telling them of the short-term joys of LSD. (I except the hippies, for from what I hear they are sick of a too materialistic, subhuman civilization and turn to love and love potions—little Tristrams and Iseults—and they like "to throw roses, roses riotously in the throng.") Where the Church has failed is not in its ideal, but in getting the modern generation to pay any attention. A boy at school will not listen to what the teacher is saying about Vergil when there is a fight going on outside the window. In early and medieval times the Church had almost a monopoly in providing attractions—processions, pictures, stained glass and frescoes which told exciting Bible stories, hymns and ecclesiastical music, and morality plays. The Mass itself stood out as a drama before great dramatists like Shakespeare purged the audiences' passions by tragedy and comedy. The holidays centered around feasts of the Church, Christmas and the New Year, the coming of the Magi, Lady Day, the coming of Spring and Maytime, the four seasons of the year. The cathedral or church was a forum and market center, and here the revels took place which had no rival except in the tavern songs of the university students. A simpler form of existence—that explains much; and now the schools for the most part have not even the dramatic symbol of the Cross on the walls, and the religious guilds and livery companies have passed into trades unions which know not their patron saints. The simple forms of drama and entertainment have become dulled by contrast with the sensational amusements young and old can now turn to in every city. The quiet muttering and intonations of the Mass or Evensong once loved have yielded their vigor to the noise of stadiums and nightclubs. The pious stories of a saint's life gather dust while crowds gather to see in the theater or on the screen *Becket* and *A Man for All Seasons*. Would that all plays had such kinds of theme! Inevitably moneymaking concerns pander to this craze for constant excitements. Nothing must be heavy or too long. Walter Scott's *Ivanhoe* appears as a booklet of seventy pages, and somehow or other the works of a Tolstoy or a Proust must be made to have the spice and excitement of an Ian Fleming. This change it is, I believe, which is responsible for the decline of churchgoing. Modern impressionism rules, and the new forms of entertainment have stolen the minds and hearts of our generation. The result is an indifference to religious faith which rarely deserves the title of skepticism. It is so easy now—until tragedy strikes or threat of war—to live from day to day with a monotonous employment of some hours listlessly or ambitiously carried out in shops and factories, for the remaining time to be spent in mindless jamborees, the newspaper, the radio or TV, the football stadiums; the faces coming nearer and nearer as the years pass to those of a complete nonentity. Nonentities do at times pass muster for humanists!

There remains one philosophy of life, a positive and challenging one, which is opposed to religion and yet reckons itself, with as much passion as the Moslem, to be the sole true form of human living. To outsiders it appears to

lack many of the features we expect in a rounded humanism; but that does not prevent it from being a seductive
voice to many. A view which has now as many as a thousand million adherents cannot be treated as of trivial importance, even though it tends to make a solitude—destroying all its enemies ruthlessly—and to call it peace.
Monolithic in structure, it is so unswerving in its proselyt-
ism that it has become a kind of bogey to the free world;
the Antichrist of the Gospels. There are some, however,
who say that we must face reality and come to terms with
communism. Their argument varies. One, a little cynical
perhaps, does use a specious logic. It assumes that willy-
nilly, human society is moving into a closer and closer
unity, economically and socially. So international now is
the financial market and so vast and complicated are the
economic measures each country has to take that authority
is forced on governments, even when they profess liberal
policies; so that each nation is turning into a state-con-
trolled society. Democracy is steadily becoming socialism,
and the form socialism takes is no different from that of
communism, except that the latter is dedicated to revolutionary measures when useful. With all the means of production in the hands of the state and the principle of complete equality finally triumphing, the nations of the world
will become indistinguishable. This analysis conforms with
the Marxist, for in it the so-called "open society," which
will promote the liberal and humanist ideal, is only a superstructure temporarily devised and of no greater importance than the older superstructures in the periods of feu-
dalism and capitalism.

To those who are lured by this one aspect of modern
culture and civilization, this conclusion seems incontro-
vertible. And if they include humanists, then humanists
must grin and bear it. But those of us who do not regard
economic man as an adequate summary of our human nature can here come to the aid of the humanist. The human-

ist has already borrowed so many plumes from Christianity that he ought to be glad of further reminders of the many-sided character of man. Economics is only an abstraction, the singling out of one human activity. There are other urges and activities, and it is because of the conflict of these desires that free will is made possible. Man looks before and after, and can sit in judgment on his own motivation as well as that of others. A Marxist has to be a complete determinist, accepting the descriptive slogan that freedom means "consciousness of necessity," or else he must modify the analysis just given. If he does not, then he will be found constantly contradicting himself. His language when attacking enemies has meaning only if the foes are really to blame; his exhortations again to the proletariat show a discrepancy between theory and act, for in act the proletariat is told to behave itself and show its ability to be virtuously Marxist, as if it could be anything else. Indeed, the Communist defies the evidence of our human experience in reducing all human ideals and aims to a single one, and that not one of the highest. History shows man as religious, artistic, imaginative, a *Homo ludens* as well as a *Homo economicus*. When Francis Chichester started to sail around the world in his *Gipsy Moth,* he had no economic aims, and nothing would have been changed had he failed. If the Marxist retorts that such individual acts can make no difference to the all-in-all of economic necessity, any more than microcosmic uncertainty in nature affects the macrocosmic theorizing and planning of the scientist, the answer is a flat denial. As compared with inanimate nature, man is not only conscious of the fixed, uniform movements around him: he directs what is necessitated to different purposes, so various that he has to make a choice between them; he can use nuclear physics for industrial or warlike purposes, or experiment out of pure interest or for fun, and suddenly abandon the uses and processes he has already begun. The discovery of the computer, for instance, is bound to affect the future of men and women, and yet it is conceivable that it need not do so, for man might make a self-denying ordinance, as he did with poison gas, and, please God, will do with nuclear bombs. The discoveries in astrophysics open vast new possibilities, but no one can even guess what choices future men will make. If we turn to ideals and ideas such as Liberty, Equality, and Fraternity, we are at a still further distance from the world of necessity and communism. The three ideals or principles do not easily fit together, and so it is left to statesmen and parties to choose which they prefer. The emphasis on equality in some countries has clearly led to a loss of liberty. Liberty again may work against fraternity, when in its name license is given to the sale of pernicious foods, drinks, and drugs, and when on television or on the stage the living as well as the dead can be slandered. It is not fraternal to keep down, so as to be on an equality with oneself, those who are far more gifted and soon to be ready, if given the opportunity, to confer some great benefit on society.

Returning to Marxism again, we can reasonably maintain that there are workable alternatives to communism. The liberal, whether in his American or English format, is still very much alive and kicking; the conservative, as representing the democracy of the dead and ancestral piety, may always be with us. When Mussolini began his hegemony he talked the language of the corporate state. As thought out by Don Sturzo, it seemed, before being tried, to be feasible. But it was never tried, because power corrupted Mussolini and induced him to convert his first intentions into a fascist tyranny. Ramiro de Maetzu gave a very attractive picture of a possible corporate society in his *Man, Function and Society*. Less attractive, but perhaps more likely and practical, is James Burnham's *Managerial Society*. Here there would be efficiency, but considerable modifications would have to be introduced if liberals were still to have their proper place.

Marxism had really one plausible claim to be the humanism of the future. It rested on the assumption that it would be the sole candidate. Once this assumption is known to be false, we can ignore it, and thank God that there are other possibilities for the future besides that of Orwell's *1984* and Aldous Huxley's *Brave New World.* Even polished up to look its best, it will not do. Its philosophy is called "dialectical materialism." A convict in Alcatraz wrote a poem which he called *The Egotist.* It ran as follows: "I looked in the mirror. Gee! it's me!" Now materialism looking at itself and arguing for its truth is a far stranger procedure than that of the convict. But more immediately to the point is the case of the word "dialectic." "Dialectic" is used generally for a discussion, an argument between persons of opposite views. In Plato it has a special sense, and it is at the core of Hegel's view of mind. The mind works by a process of denying an affirmative, and out of the opposition arriving at a richer idea. There is a thesis, then an antithesis, and from them a synthesis. That this is at any rate one of the ways in which the mind works in developing its thought is apparent to all. But it needed the genius of a Marx to make this thought process look good when transferred to material processes. Hegel was an idealist, that is, he believed nature was what he called an "objective idea"—in other words, latent thought, what in fact can and will be expressed in thought. Marx denied this; he reduced thought to material reality and identified the dialectic with the struggle for existence. They are really quite different, though they have resemblances. The scientists treat of positive and negative units, such as protons and electrons, and amongst living things there are changes which can metaphorically be called "dialectical." When we reach man's estate owing to the presence and activity of mind, dialectic, though a stranger to what is happening, does serve to illustrate social and economic developments. Marx, however, takes it as an ultimate principle which is at work in forming class divisions. Men use others, and by so doing gradually undermine their own position and authority; and throughout history the social order is said to contain within it the germs of its own destruction and renewal. In the final resort man attains a condition in which there is no longer any class, and so the dialectic, having nothing to work on, comes to an end. Throughout this dialectic of history there is a confusion between the dialectic of ideas and the conflict of opposing forces in nature and in man. In evolution the operative words are "survival of the fittest." This in turn is a generalization which calls for more accurate or specific explanations in the concrete. Its virtue lies in its being a negative norm, just as a turnstile keeps out those who have no tickets. It does not tell us, however, what the tickets are for, whether for a football game or drama or musical festival. Recruits for the army with weak chests may be rejected, although they have already succeeded brilliantly in university examinations and been accepted on a university faculty.

The most illuminating generalization is, I think, that of challenge—one already touched on above, where I referred to the disintegration of the muscles and organs of the body when they meet no resistances or challenge. The advantage of this generalization is that it is so well exemplified in human life. As our teeth and stomach, which were developed to chew and digest hard mastodon meat, deteriorate when the food is soft and creamy, so the five senses and the imagination lose their power when they are not well exercised. Too often we see a young man with an exceptional mind gradually turn into an uninteresting bore, because of laziness. Human beings never come to know themselves and appreciate their own powers unless they compete with others in games and studies and law courts and parliaments. The myths are right in pointing to the lame god, the hero with a wound. So universal is this need of a challenge that one is tempted to say that Satan, the Adversary, would have to be invented if he did not already exist, so necessary a part does he play in the historic drama of man. Looking back on the past we see how the self-indulgent races decline; stagnation sets in and they sleep the sleep of death or are stamped out by invaders. Marx is exploiting this truth in his theory of dialectical necessity, and he has no right to dispense with it in his earthly paradise, the golden age to come of the classless society. Such a society would sit about in a Lotus land, listless in a subhuman life little better than that of a vegetable. Even the Christian philosopher and sociologist, who plans and prays for a universal society, happy and at peace, has to get around the problem of the challenge. Heaven is another matter, for there the problem is solved by the change of our human condition. Time is no more and we are to be lifted up and energized by an immortal love, which gives us more than our heart's content. But human life shows no signs of turning into the state of bliss called heaven, so we still have to wonder what humanism can do for us and what form it should take.

The Marxist ideal, and indeed all secular forms of humanism, have another criticism to face. It has already been mentioned, and Ayer did not hide its gravity. Virginia Woolf expressed it and showed how it affected a delicate, withdrawn spirit like her own. "Life had been imperfect, an unfinished phrase. It had been impossible for me, taking snuff as I do from any bagman met in a train, to keep coherency—that sense of the generations, of women carrying pitchers to the Nile, of the nightingale who sings among conquests and migrations." The gravamen is that life is an "unfinished phrase" at its best and at its worst a nightmare. The individual has but a short stay, and one which often he cannot control. He may be born into misery or cushioned into softness. He has to take his chance with friends and with all whom he meets; his choices are in the dark, his loves uncertain, his own powers of body and mind unreliable. He has to creep when he would fly, labor when he would play; he is tantalized by the promises of a better life, of a world of truth and an empire of love, and he never hears more than the first bars of the symphony. Every unreligious explanation has so far had to leave so much out. Marx, for example, seemed untroubled by the fact that he reserved full satisfaction of life to a generation still to come. Thousands of years have been spent and millions upon millions of human beings have been shut out from the promised land. Their lives are of no account except as the slaves were of account who built the pyramids. As the Psalmist says, they sowed but they did not reap, and their personal tragedies will never have an emended and joyous ending. Such an outlook is doctrinaire and prejudiced and makes nothing of the mysterious interdependence of mankind. Donne's famous saying that no man is an island, "any man's death diminishes me, because I am involved in mankind," is one which no humanist can ignore. In other respects, too, Marxism gives too short a measure; for we take it as a sorry view of our humanity when the best plan we can see for it is to force total socialization on individual persons. To be at the beck and call of the state in everything that is important, this is to return to a harmless serfdom. It is also a mean and short-sighted view of man.

This indifference to the fate of the multitudes living and dead is not peculiar to Communists: it is shared by oligarchs[2] such as the once well-known Bloomsbury group, which included the Woolfs, Roger and Vanessa Fry, Lytton Strachey, and others, with Lord Keynes and Lord (Bertrand) Russell coming and going. Their recipe for good living owed much to the philosopher G. E. Moore and to Lowes Dickinson. They admired beauty, whether visual, musical, or written, and were drawn together by similar tastes or similar background, and they experienced a

[2] I say "oligarchs" not autocrats, because the aristocratic ideal is one of service, not of refined enjoyment.

heightened sense of living in the warmth of friendship and good talk. Being none of them religious believers, they found a substitute for this in friendship and good taste. They shut off the noise of the world. They were not like St. Patrick, who heard at night the cry of the simple people. "The children from Focluth by the Western sea, who cried out to him: 'O holy youth, come back to us and walk once more amongst us.'" Let it be said, however, to their honor that they bore without rage or bitterness the loss of children and friends who went crusading for causes they thought just.

Conscience and good judgment forbid us to identify humanism and pleasure, though there clearly ought to be some connection. Over and over again this matter has been discussed by Plato and Aristotle, Stoic and hedonist, Christian and freethinker. There is no reason, therefore, to start the argument over again, especially as there is a common consent now that a human being is incomplete if he isolates himself from the welfare of others. The ideal is not to be found in some coterie or class. Pleasure, as I say, is normally an ingredient of the good life, but the pleasure we enjoy cannot be at the expense of others. It has been said with justice that whatever we are doing we ought to be able to do it with a clear conscience so that not even the hardest hit or unfortunate could rightly point a finger of accusation at us. A better word than independence is interdependence, for men cannot and ought not to seek to do without each other. As well as interdependence a degree of wisdom is required. The simple often have by nature a grace, but the average educated man can be distressingly limited in his sympathies and understanding because his mind is stunted. As each of us is a miniature Atlas carrying the world on our shoulders, we ought to know something of the nature and value of that world. In this context it is useful to make a distinction, and one form of it is that between the certain and the true (*certum et verum*). The items of the day and of our upbringing and our experience make up our certainties. We are quite sure that X wronged Y, that we bought a kitten yesterday, that we have a limited amount of money, that we can talk fairly well on a few subjects and are very ignorant of others—and much of this kind of knowledge will center around our profession or business or employment. Some of these certainties, as I have already pointed out, are absolute: we have a body and senses and a mind, we had parents, we meet many who are human like ourselves as well as live beings who are different; we are aware too of vices and virtues, of political and social improvements, and we consciously or unconsciously have our own point of view. In coming to have a point of view we come to the "true," the *verum*. I keep this word *verum* for what is more panoramic. We are all philosophers in embryo, and we have to listen to others giving us their point of view, their summaries of what the world is or should be, and we ourselves usually have something of our own to say. Here it is all important to have an open mind, not that that means an undecided chameleon or Vicar of Bray mind: it is rather one that is always responsive to new ideas and sympathetic even in disagreement. There are some who are too lazy to ask questions or afraid to do so; they do not escape, however, by burying their heads in the sand, for this very action is a declaration of a belief, and this belief will be either a truth—a *verum*—or a lie. The *verum* then shows our frame of mind, our personal response to the problems that arise when questions are forced upon us, when the crises cannot be avoided, when we have to know where we stand. Above all our journeyman certainties ought to be consistent one with another and to meet on a background of truth. How perplexing it is and defeatist if we have to own that our moral beliefs have in fact no cosmic basis, that our idea of liberty is incompatible with our accepted view of the universe, and that there is no relation between our daily certainties and the philosophical position we feel bound to hold. To put the matter more plainly and correctly: let us suppose a man is educated to have a high sense of responsibility and regard for other persons, with a strict conscience about promises made and honesty in his work, and then he is driven to believe from his reading or by the persuasive arguments of a modern philosopher that the language about the soul and free will and immortality is mistaken; that morality is a convention and that he is foolish to try to make sense of life and think out a coherent view of life. There is an unbridgeable gap between his certainties and what can be called a framework into which these certainties ought to fit. To state this in still another way, the Curé d'Ars, a very simple saint of the nineteenth century, to whom over 50,000 pilgrims a year used to come in his last years, once remarked about a skeptical philosopher, "How can he be thought wise when he does not know where he came from or where he is going?"

The modern secular humanists escape from this quandary by saying we can be well content with theories of life which work. To seek for absolutes or ultimates or answers beyond the grave is a waste of time. Lord Francis-Williams tells his hearers on television that humanism is a form of life which finds no need of absolutes or supernatural explanations. All is well if we move ahead with a limited certainty about a certain number of things. (A woman with that kind of certainty found that she had got into a plane for Chicago when her destination was Honolulu.) I should like to have seen a Socrates interviewing him. He prefers openmindedness to absolutes. But why should a system of absolutes not be the answer if one's mind is really open? Openmindedness can, as we know in practice, end in finality. It is good to have an ending to a story or a journey. It would seem that his mind is as closed as that of the theo-logian, for it is closed to the arguments and conclusions of many great philosophers, to the exhortations of saints and mystics, to dramatists and poets like Aeschylus and Dante.

He is undisturbed by the problems of pain, moral evil, and death, but open to some strange, godlike, moving shape called evolution; for he goes on to say that we must walk in the belief that, so far as we can see, Man (with a capital letter) is the chief agent and the highest expression of the evolutionary principle. Insofar as he has any dedication it is to help forward that force of evolution. Such a resolution or sentiment may merit a cheer, but it comes near to being meaningless. Philosophers are chary of talking about such an abstraction as evolution, and have to unpack it before putting it into any proposition which could be judged true or false; scientists use it in a specific sense according to the subject matter they are dealing with, and even then it serves not as a treasured truth so much as a much-needed hypothesis. When we do try to give it a general meaning it ceases to be very worshipful—less so than the sun, which shines on the good and bad: for nature while it gets rid of the unfit does in the process much that is lovely and precious. In averting his gaze from absolutes Lord Francis-Williams seems to have fallen in love with a monster.

This is not to deny that it is pleasant at times to give up thinking; to doubt, perhaps, whether philosophizing or looking for final causes can add a jot to our living. Do not many empiricists refuse to bother with anything they cannot weigh or taste or see or feel? Let the old wise men of Gotham set out in their tub, we can rest on our oars and laugh at them. Insanity this may not be, but it is a kind of mental cataract, for there are millions who do not laugh, millions who are forced by the nature of their experience to cry out for answers. These find a voice in the modern existentialists, who loathe that too complacent bourgeois attitude which closes its eyes to the agonies of the spirit, to man's individual loneliness, the persistent sense of responsibility, and the grim specter which makes all futile, namely, death. We are in so many ways better off than our ancestors, but their minds were more open—to repeat that

word—to the problems which beset the human person—
the purpose of one's life, evil, sin, and death. Even the very
simple knew of them by what has been called "a kind of
cultural osmosis. Philosophical conclusions, doctrinal
meanings, reached them through ceremony and sermon,
custom and observance."

That there must be answers the young are fain to believe, but the old, it may be said—and by the old one can
mean also the present generation, which is old in its civilization—have learned the sad lesson that philosophizing has
in fact constantly failed man. Philosophers do little more
than prove each other wrong: they have heated brains and
cold feet and their recommendations seldom heal the ills of
mankind. Therefore let us eat and be merry and sad in
life's ups and downs, making the best of it. Philosophers, I
think, should strike their breasts, but all the same the
world would be a worse place without the wisdom of a
Pythagoras, a Plato, or an Aristotle, to mention only the
Greeks. Perhaps, too, it was asking too much of them to
provide the key to the world's mystery. It may be that it is
only religion which can open the book that is "written
within and without and sealed with seven seals." Human
learning, honest and high-minded as it can be, does look at
times like a dusty answer. Professor Anthony Flew of Keele
University in a talk for the B.B.C. tackled this problem,
"Does Morality Pay?" His conclusion was that the attempts
of Socrates in Plato's *Republic* to show that it does failed,
for in the world of our experience morality manifestly does
not always pay; it may even demand the sacrifice of our
happiness. At the same time he gives his argument a
strange twist in the following words: "It is perverse to try
to make out that it always pays to be just. It does not. It is
also demoralizing: such attempts must tend to devalue the
sometimes authentically sacrificial devotion of good and
dutiful people into a mere enlightened self-interest." This
is a fair example of an attempt to face a human problem

without any reference to religion or an afterlife. Flew from his writings shows that he is unable to believe in God or in the Christian faith. That being so, he has, I think, an easy task in proving that time and again morally good actions do not bring success or happiness. On a national scale, England's action in going to the aid of Belgium in the First World War and in challenging the aggressions of Hitler in the Second World War has not paid. Many of its best citizens sacrificed themselves by death, and by its Pyrrhic victories England is now in a crisis. Why then be dutiful? The problem falls under the distinctions already made between the certain (*certum*) and the true (*verum*). The problem does not seem to have an answer, if an act of duty brings no immediate happiness in a meaningless universe. The humanist—and here in his language Flew seems to be of their company—tries to escape the difficulty by appealing to an intrinsic value in being dutiful independent of any further consideration. This is what I have called the "certainty": we know we are doing right and we have a peace and satisfaction in so acting. Flew puts this almost paradoxically by suggesting that "a sacrificial devotion" stands by itself and to ask anything more is to descend into "enlightened self-interest." But this will not do. When we say that duty pays we ought not to have in mind an "enlightened self-interest." Only the hedonist means and must mean that. It is quite a different philosophy which says there must be some connection between our ultimate aim in life and doing our duty. One might say even that doing one's duty could have no meaning were there no connection, even as one could say that a full and perfect life in society would be thwarted by a habit of telling lies. Here the duty of telling the truth and the good which comes of it are plainly seen. If, however, no good came to one or to society in being dutiful, duty would tend to become meaningless. When we say that duty is its own reward, we take for granted a universe in which duty and good have some relation. If, however, we conclude that life is meaningless or that we can make no sense of the world, will duty continue to have a meaning and be its own reward? A mindful act in a mindless universe. The humanist may still protest that an act of duty of its very nature gives us peace and satisfaction even though it costs us dearly. But this is flagrantly untrue; duties performed can at times give no pleasure or satisfaction. Nursing an ungrateful and bad-tempered invalid or paying a debt to one who is likely to use the money in ways which will hurt both ourselves and others whom we like—these and many other cases could be quoted, where we feel the obligation to be an imposition and not a pleasure. Again, if onerous duties multiplied by geometric progression life might well become intolerable —in an indifferent universe.

But even granted that a sufferer can say to himself, "I will make the best of it," and go on gallantly, what of the general picture? What do we think of a world where so many duties are imposed and millions suffer and have no reward? Why observe rules when the world begins to gape wide with irrationality? It often happens that a son or daughter has to look after an invalid parent, and so lose opportunities to follow his or her own bent: at times it may mean the sacrifice of a career and of great potential talent. Conscience has kept them at home, and therefore they believe that they are certainly acting rightly. But this certainty is left hanging in the air if there be no philosophy of life to give it a place and function. That philosophy need not be thought out, for it is likely that the majority of people treat life as if it had some purpose, possibly taking refuge in some adage such as "All is for the best" or that "There are more things in heaven and earth, Horatio, than are dreamt of in your philosophy."

The fact that such odd sayings serving for wisdom are on the lips of most men and women is evidence that every experience of the good or the dutiful has a tale to tell also of a world of good, as the pleasure felt by a baby girl at the sight of a doll is a presentiment of maternal love. Certainties stand by themselves, but they are not isolated; they are themselves instructions as to what the world is like, and they save us from regarding the universe as a bedlam in which the good suffer in vain and the evil can riotously pay no attention to the law.[3]

In the stories told to children there has to be a happy ending. Evil is defeated, the prince wins his beloved, and they live happily ever after. This inborn belief suffers many shocks: it is queried by the existentialists, and the modern humanists would have us ignore it. For them there are no absolutes, no final meaning; there is no Perseus to slay the Medusa and rescue Andromeda, and death has the last word. Such a humanism looks inhuman. Its last whisper is *Heu! lacrymae rerum!* and not that God "shall wipe away all tears."

---

[3] In support of what I am saying, I have, as I am glad to read and to know, the views expressed by Bertrand Russell as a young man in his *Autobiography:* "Nothing can penetrate it (the loneliness of the human heart) except the highest intensity of the sort of love the religious teachers have preached. Whatever does not spring from this motive is harmful and at best useless. . . . Seriously the unmystical rationalistic view of life seems to omit all that is most important and most beautiful." I am glad that Lord Russell has never forsaken this mystical view of life.

CHAPTER 3

THE SECULAR
CITY

The world awakes to a new year 1968, but it is unaware that it is A.D.

Fra Angelico's *Coronation of the Virgin* was once hung in the checkroom at the Louvre.

When the sun has risen we know this not by staring at it, but because we can see everything else clearly.

Having examined humanism as it appears to the modern rationalist, existentialist, and others, its strength and weakness, we have now to try to find out whether religion and specifically Christianity has anything to contribute. The secularists answer in the negative, and great sympathy with this point of view was expressed, as we have seen, by Dietrich Bonhoeffer. Time has brought its revenges, and whereas in the fifth century St. Augustine felt it imperative to make a division between the City of God and the City of Man, and to argue that the decline of the Roman Empire was due to its own secular weaknesses and not to the practice of the Beatitudes, now it is the secular city which grows stronger and stronger, and religion which looks to be tapering out. To repeat the well-known diagnosis of Bonhoeffer, this phenomenon is due to the maturity of man. He is now no longer in swaddling clothes or needing a governess and a pedagogue: he stands on his own feet, and this should be applauded by the Christian. Religion as a separate form of life can well disappear, because "God is teaching us that we must live as men who can get along very well without Him." As the early Christians gave up circumcision, so we have to give up a kind of garment called religion.

These letters of Bonhoeffer seem to have been astonishingly opportune, so rapturously have they been accepted, and widely proclaimed. So many have said, "This is what I wanted to hear, and how true it is!" But as usually happens in certain quarters, the good news has been interpreted in an extreme fashion. Not only must the word "religion" be bracketed, but also the name of God. A number of writers in America, four in particular, have been grouped under one umbrella. They are the "death of God" theologians. Of their wisdom or extravagances there is no need here to say anything, except insofar as their views bear on humanism. They believe that we are living in a post-Christian culture, and they feel deeply committed to this culture, especially in its American form. It is by various means that they dispose of God. T. L. J. Altizer, for example, is influenced by the Hegelian dialectic of history, and therefore he holds that God has ceased to be God in becoming a man, Jesus. The Incarnation is the death of God in His divine being, it effects the "absolute negation of the primordial or essential being of God." But the presence of Jesus, though God died with Jesus on the Cross, does in a sense make up for this, and our culture will only be fully human by Christ's transfiguring Word, which will finally bring it about that somehow or other God "will be all in all." Humanism, as possessing the spirit of Christianity without a theology, is apparent in this view. Gabriel Vahanian is more elusive in his thought and perhaps more suggestive. He is antisecularist and regards God not as necessary but as inevitable. By that I think he means that though we are losing the sense of the presence of God, our culture would be a "chimera" without Christ. "We have domesticated the Universe, or so we think, but we have lost the cipher of its symbols: we have estranged ourselves from it." Such a statement, I fancy, could be used by the secular or the Christian humanist. William Hamilton, for his part, says that "there is in us the death of any power to affirm the traditional image of God." This is a broad statement, and it could imply a failure on man's part plus a neutral attitude as to God's existence. There is no doubt that he vacillates, and he would classify himself rather as an ex-atheist than as an atheist. It is his desire to be quite free from religious obligations and to identify himself with modern culture, "From Prufrock to Ringo," which makes him a Mr. Looking-Both-Ways. He ought really to see how deeply affected by Christianity and committed to its culture the Western world is.

The chief idea lying behind the arguments of these critics is that whether we like it or not modern culture can get on very well without recourse to God. Religious language is now irrelevant. "Our lives," as Emerson W. Shideler says in *The Meaning of the Death of God,* "are no longer in the hand of God but in the hands of medical technologists and the research specialists who are seeking cures of the fatal diseases which still take us off." As another critic, Edward B. Fiske, writes: "Christian symbols no longer permeate society, belief in God is no longer felt to be a necessary operating hypothesis, and those in the pews on Sunday morning often operate as if God were indeed dead" (*The New York Times,* April 22, 1966).

This schism remarked on by these writers is worldwide, but their experience is drawn from America, where necessarily the roots of Christianity cannot go so deep. Probably they think that in Europe Christianity died long ago, for how otherwise interpret the question asked so brashly by Michael Novak, "Can Christianity absorb the sudden irrelevance of the categories of European Christendom and transform its own basic insights and expectations into the language of the American experience?" All the hope these writers can at present offer their fellow countrymen is that Christianity as still alive in the figure of Christ may serve as a profane presence in a world gone completely secular. The word of life is that "God is dead and Jesus is his son."

Harvey Cox has been quoted alongside this group of writers, but he is in a different league. He does not believe that the day of religion and Christianity is over. In some passages he writes as if he were a Bible Christian. It is his distinction to have caught the ear of the young and old, even as the Beatles became the voices of their own generation. Cox's work is far and away the most plausible effort to bring religion up to date and to spell it out in the language of contemporary urban society. The test of this is in the large sales of his book *The Secular City* and the demand for him to lecture all over the United States. As contrasted with those humanists hitherto criticized, Cox holds that Christianity is definitely alive and that its future lies in its identification with the secular city. Humanism has absorbed religion to its good. He can be counted with Bishop Robinson and W. Hamilton as calling for a new Christian way of life, that is, quite at ease with all that goes on in a city, where motorcars, radios, subways, skyscrapers, and the rest of the modern paraphernalia abound. As a modern critic has written, here is "the question of a new style of the technical expert trained to solve specific problems requiring a definite 'know-how' that is contrasted with the more traditional style of the theological synthesis and the general 'know-why'." Cox claims that his view is Biblical, that, like Bishop Robinson's *Honest to God,* it faces fairly and squarely what is happening in man's evolution. He lays great stress on history and the historical process, for man is alive in history and determined by his history. He is convinced that there has always been a more or less strict correlation between the economic level and the supernatural structure, the kind of beings postulated by the feelings of the tribe or individual. Far back in history where tribal life predominated, the shaman represented the tribe's religious reactions to its surroundings, when he danced and sang and initiated the tribe's identification with its daimon. The same correlation is present between economy and religion in the story of Yankee puritanism. Now conditions have changed and rapidly: urbanization has grown apace, and the townsman has different problems from those of his more countrified ancestors.

Cox has no high opinion of past Christian theology. It looks to him like a constant attempt to resist and dilute the radical Biblical drive and genius. The explanation which he gives for this is the infiltration of Greek thought. The Bible itself is bursting with life and history, but the Christian religion was soon wrapped up in unhistorical metaphysical abstractions. Time was supplanted by space, and temporal images by spatial ones; the success of the medieval theological synthesis was bought at a price, for it resolved the tension between Hebrew and Greek thought by making the spatial world the more important and religious one, while the changing world of history was relegated to a lower place and called "secular." If we are to believe Cox and his interpretation of Bonhoeffer, the early Church was healthily down to earth. It displayed a kind of "holy-worldliness"; the reason why the early Christians rejected the cults of Cybele, Isis, and Mithras was that these were escapist, mystery religions which were not sufficiently of the world.

Such a bad start would have ruined the case of many another writer, but Cox improves as he goes on. He is at one with Bonhoeffer in holding that man has now reached the parting of the ways. Tobias grown up will have no archangel; the Dantes must do without their Beatrices. No longer can man depend on supernatural help. "Not only his language, his customs, his clothing style, but also his science, his values and his very way of perceiving reality are conditioned by his personal biography and the history of his group." Values no longer exist: we have only valuations, and secular man knows that the symbols by which he perceives the world and the values are not out there independently of him. They are the products of a particular history. Even moral values must go into the melting pot. That, however, is not as disastrous as it seems: for with the relativization of values more constructive results can be achieved. We can recognize that since everyone's perspective is limited and conditioned, no one has the right to inflict his values on anyone else. If one cries out that this logically means bedlam and licensed—if the word now has any meaning—immorality, he says, "Not at all," for that is to talk like an adolescent. We must think and behave like grown-ups.

Our world, in Cox's view, is approximating more and more to a secular city, with a shape of its own and a culture of its own. The social system gives it its shape, and the images of this social system are in brief the switchboard and the highway cloverleaf; that is to say, the image of simultaneous mobility in many different directions. The secular city, according to a common complaint, bulldozes what is private and personal: it is necessarily anonymous. Cox agrees, but counters by saying that anonymity and mobility[1] have a liberating influence. We needs must have supermarkets, air service, and cafeterias: in order to survive we have to adopt a hedgehog attitude. But this has its compensations; it serves as a challenge. "In the historical process itself man meets the One who calls him into being as a free deciding self and knows that neither his past history nor his environment determines what he does." In the anonymity of urban culture, far from the fishbowl of town life, modern man experiences both the terror and the delight of human freedom more acutely. It is in the modern social

[1] Though Biblical in intent, Cox bulldozes St. Paul; for instance, "Therefore, my dearly beloved, be ye steadfast, unmoveable" (I Cor. 15:58).

mix-up that the Biblical God is perceived, and the law and the Gospel give us the means of understanding secular events, including urbanization. Our confidence in the future of this multifarious, mechanized, and computer world rests upon the God of the Gospel, who has insisted on our need to exercise freedom and responsibility.

With this anonymity in the modern city goes an increase of mobility. Think of the girl at the telephone exchange, the man at the switchboard, the driver at the packed intersection. Other images are of the airport control tower, the high-speed elevators, and the escalators now a part of every large store. (I cannot resist interrupting—for some of the modern inventions chosen are for the sake of immobility. The telephone saves walking, the elevator saves climbing, and Cox might as well have chosen the mobile chair which some golfers use to save them from walking around the golf course!) Such mobility enables people at the bottom to rise and raise their status; it leads to a true equality and frees us from the static, spatial world we have been accustomed to. What is more, our idea of God is improved, for in his despatialization God can be seen to be active in historical events. So captivated at this point is Cox by his own distinction between space and time, the static and the mobile, that he assures us that "the early Church's belief in the Ascension can be read as a refusal to allow its Lord to be localized or spatially restricted. The Ascension in its simplest terms means that Jesus is mobile." Later, so we learn from him, "the medieval Church allowed the Christian Gospel to be changed into a Baal cult, and it was not until the missionary movement of the nineteenth century and the ecumenical movement of the twentieth that the mistaken notions of Christendom began to disappear." I cannot help wondering what the medieval St. Francis of Assisi would have thought of the Baal cult. I doubt if he heard of it even when he went as a missionary to Damietta and the Holy Land.

So far Harvey Cox has been drawing the shape of the secular city. He now goes on to treat of its style. He says that it has two characteristics, pragmatism and profanity. Metaphysics is a worn-out business, and nobody now is interested in it. We ask instead, does a thing work? Again, there is no longer any interest in some supramundane[2] reality. All that supernatural stuff is no longer for sale. Nevertheless we are told rather unexpectedly that asceticism is still viable, for to be pragmatic is to be ascetic. His point is that life now in technopolis is full of problems. In place of the old up-in-the-air, theoretical ones, man is faced today with a hodgepodge of human purposes and projects, and he is conscious that all he does is provisional and relative. He faces these and is able to carry on without reliance on some trans-stellar deity because he recognizes himself as the source of whatever significance the human enterprise holds. All eternal verities are merely projections of the society in which we live. They change, he says, when the society changes, and in predictable ways. There is nothing timeless or divine about them. St. Thomas Aquinas, for example, has no message for us now, for he made the mistake of thinking that the world consisted of "a hierarchical, cosmic order fixed and finished for all time." We know now that there is no ordered universe awaiting the discovery of it by man. The universe itself is a human invention. All this goes to show that the old problems, including the religious one, do not occur to the newly emergent, urban, secular man. "They arise in fact not from the structures of existence at all, but from the erosion of inherited world views and cultural meanings."

Despite all his criticism of the past religious philosophy and outlook, Cox does not plump for any secularist world view. He would like, I believe, to be thought of as a Bible

2 "For thee, O dear, dear country, mine eyes their vigils keep; for very love beholding thy happy name, they weep." Translation of Bernard de Morlaix.

Christian alive to what is happening now. He distinguishes secularization, as a historical movement, which he advocates, from secularism as an ideology, and surely this is a valuable distinction if he can keep to it. To his mind only the first of these two is a liberating process. The liberating process, however, comes from man himself and must be arduous and painful. Here the example of Christ is to the point, for his action was historical. His initiative and human responses were directed to promote the coming of the kingdom. "The coming of the Kingdom of God in Christ coincided with man's laying aside precious values and loyalties and freely entering the new reality." It was revolutionary action, and all theology if it is to mean anything must be revolutionary and exhibit certain definite features. These features Cox sums up in four words. First, "catalytic." This covers the explanation of why action is needed, and precisely practical action. Second, "catalepsy." This explains why so many people prefer to do nothing. Third, "catharsis." This shows how people can be changed; and, lastly, "catastrophe." The word tells its tale—a tale of the overturning of tables, the removal of dead wood, and newness of life.

This change has to be preceded by an interim or gap because man is slow to see his needs, and he likes to stay with the easily understood and the conventional. He is upset by crisis in the economic world and by his inability to master unemployment, bad housing, and road problems. Technopolis is not an easy cup to drink. In the interim before action the problem seems impossible, and this brings with it a sense of sin or guilt. "He is like," says Cox, "a person living in a trance induced by post-hypnotic suggestion." The Bible describes his state by figures such as lameness, deafness, sleep, and death. There is only one cure, which goes by the name of *metanoia,* a new change of mind and heart, which has been usually translated by the word "repentance." Man is now uprooted from traditional sources of value, and urbanization expresses his human effort "to come to terms with the new historical reality, the formulation of ways to live more equably with other human beings in a system of increasing reciprocity."

In this last sentence is the core of Harvey Cox's attempt to reconstitute together Christianity and modern life, and it is worthwhile pondering over it. He dismisses much that Christians think important as secondary. Doctrines, for instance, only come as an afterthought, after, that is, man has already started, in cooperation with God, to bring about the secular kingdom. The function of the Church has, therefore, to be revised. "It has no plan for rebuilding the world. It has only the signal to flash that the One who frees slaves and summons men to maturity is still in business." We should not turn away from the problems of the secular city as if it, the Church, could save us from the impact of economic forces, or miraculously, without our doing anything, end social injustice. "Religion is in a sense the neurosis of culture: secularization corresponds to maturation, for it signifies the emancipation of man first from religion and then from metaphysical control." All that we have and all that we need is given to us in technopolis. It provides the technical and social basis for the emancipation of work, for a changeover from drudgery to a delight in work. (Interrupting his argument again, I have to say that I cannot see how drudgery can be avoided unless electronic machines and computers leave the workman nothing to do except enter a monastery and contemplate God.) In the old days he who did not delve got no pay or help from the state. Nowadays all is changed, what with automation and cybernetics, the sciences of control and feedback systems. Economics, like politics, are created by human artifice; they can be altered and improved. It is wrong to treat them as unchanging elements in creation and, like so-called natural laws, protected by divine sanctions. Cox holds that the central fact of modern life is that we can make enough to allow everyone to share in the goods of the earth, but the systems we now have for connecting individuals to the supply of goods is breaking down, and we are unable to alter the system because we have a semiconscious religious commitment to it. I must say in parenthesis again, that the day when all can be fed as they should must indeed be prayed for, but to write as Cox does is to ignore the very real problems which at this moment baffle the best and most generous minds. Cox may be right, though he does not prove his belief, that there could and should come a time when work is separated from market requirements. Then artists could act with full freedom and integrity and men could engage upon the work they like, and the old inveterate division between work and play, labor and leisure, would come to a timely end. But is not this implicitly to confess that technopolis, where all is cloverleaf, switchboard, and commuting, is not an ideal condition for human life? The leisure Harvey Cox craves looks more like a return to the William Morris–Eric Gill medieval idea of work than a glorification of the secular, modern city.

In these first chapters *The Secular City* seems more or less a secularist tract peppered and salted with some Biblical texts and references. In the last chapters, Cox's aim is to disclose the true import of the Christian religion in modern urban life. He warns us that we can look for God in the wrong place. God is hidden, *ex officio* hidden, and "hiddenness belongs to his nature as God." In Christ God does not cease to be hidden, "rather he meets men as the unavoidable other." But we must at all costs have done with the ideas about God which satisfied an older and different society. "The sublime firmament of overhead reality that provided a spiritual home for the souls of men until the eighteenth century has collapsed." As Amos Wilder says, "If we are to have any transcendent today, even Christian, it is to be found in the world and not overhead." I wonder why the word "transcendent" is still kept, considering that this transcendent is only present with us in social life when He is not transcendent. Poets and artists help us to see beyond "the fences of social and religious propriety" because they deal at first hand with life. (I should have thought that it was soldiers and sailors, the farmhand and the poor, who deal at first hand with life. The artists' and the poets' gifts enable them to look beyond it.) The very names given to God in the past, such as Shepherd, King, or Father, reflect the economic and social conditions of their times. Now that in the city we are perforce neighborly and work together (with the Hoffas and Reuthers?) in factory or scientific installations and unions, *alongsidedness* is the key word. In such a context it would be better to make use of an I-You relation in preference to Buber's I-Thou. The reason given for this is that the I-You relation suggests that we have God with us as a work partner. The I-Thou is perhaps a little stiff and churchy, but Cox dislikes it as belonging more to adolescent lovers. As backing for this kind of language and for making God a work partner, appeal is made to the Bible. There Yahweh is said to be more interested in justice and kindred subjects than in our aspirations and desires to see him face to face. We are even told that "Paul had little patience with the religious questions after the unknown God." What Cox means by this I do not know, considering that Paul took such immense trouble preparing his speech at the Areopagus and deliberately brought in the reference to the "unknown God." At any rate, Cox thinks that much of the loving and emotional language about God is out of date, and he seems to sympathize with those theologians who say that a God of that sort is best thought of as dead. We have to find a new name for God which will be relevant to technopolis. "Since naming is a human activity embedded in a socio-cultural milieu, there is no holy language as such, and the word 'God' is not sacred. All languages are historical. They are born and die." But is there not here a confusion between naming individuals and the names of a species? In the latter case, whether we say "lion" or speak Latin and say *"leo"* we are referring to the same object.

In short, then, Harvey Cox's view comes to this, that Christianity and the secular city can go very well together on certain conditions. These conditions will only seem hard to those who are wedded to the past, to absolutes, static doctrines, and a spatial supernaturalism. We have to accept change, especially social and cultural changes. Culture is dependent on economics, and both have to be related to the new technique of teamwork. In modern society, especially in the city, men are together and engaged, and if this engagement is to be vivified it must be in a togetherness with God in Christ. This alliance constitutes the kingdom of God in the one world we know, the human secular world. The theory of the two cities is no longer workable, nor is a separate body called the clergy needed any more. Cox seems to have an animus against ministers and priests. He writes somewhat contemptuously of them as ostrich-feathered and medicine men. "If theology is to survive and to make any sense to the contemporary world it must neither cling to a metaphysical world-view nor collapse into a mythical mode. It must push on into the living lexicon of the urban secular man."

The Secular City, as I have said, represents better than any other book I know a type of modern approach to the problem of Christianity in its relation to secular life. Secular life is looked at, and though as ugly as Anne of Cleves, is declared to be the only actual marriageable damsel around. Here is a humanism which must be accepted without any rival, but its straight course depends upon its acclaiming the Biblical down-to-earth God, who made himself, without any qualification, man. Hence its extraordinary success, and this means it deserves comment and adjudication. Cox is an American pragmatist with a noticeable streak of Marxist economic theory, who would plainly call himself a

Biblical Christian. Occasionally he borrows terminology which is Freudian, but he has little use for existentialism. He regards those who call themselves existentialists as survivors from the collapse of the middle class. They have succeeded throne and altar, and have set up opera houses and museums and suchlike bourgeois products. They are as unwanted in a technical society as the Mormons were by the Yankees. They receive no handshake from the Cox of technopolis. Existentialism is for him the last child of a cultural epoch, born in its mother's senility. That is why existentialist writers seem, to use his own word, to be so Arcadian, and I suppose we will henceforth have to think of Sartre and James Joyce, Camus and Samuel Beckett, as dwellers in Arcadia. This is perhaps because Cox is absorbed by economics and politics; hence if we want to know what God is doing in the world we must look at politics. It is politics which make and keep life human; not, I assume, the politics of a Herod or a Pilate, but the politics of technopolis. Theology figures still in the curriculum, but not as having its old function. Doctrinal theology is as dead as an Egyptian mummy. It has now the task of analyzing what we must do to keep life human in this hard-faced, metallic world of ours. Theology can do this by trying to find out what "this politician, God, is up to, and it moves in to work along with him." "We speak of God in a secular fashion when we recognize man as his partner, as the one charged with the task of bestowing meaning and order in human history."

This then is Christianity or humanism—it does not matter much which word one uses—brought up to date and dressed in a way which would be intelligible, relevant, and practical. Except for an occasional misgiving that Cox has not the faintest idea of what the worship of God means, so lacking in any numinous quality or reverence or delicacy of mind is he, I see no *a priori* reason for rejecting him wholesale. He wants to work out the ideal of the Incarnation, of God the Word becoming flesh and entering history, logically and without qualms or taking refuge in piety. He feels, I think, that he is writing in the spirit of the Bible, which is always realistic when freed from occasional Greek trimmings. Many would, I think, applaud some of the positive contribution he makes, if it could be separated from the shallow pragmatism and bad history in which it is embedded.

As it stands, however, almost everything he says is open to denial or some degree of correction. He accepts without questioning the pragmatic approach. I have already criticized this as unequal to the task of explaining even our daily certainties. Absolutes, whether in religion, morals, or philosophy, are dismissed with contempt. Probability is enough, but, as usual with deniers of absolutes, they spoil their case by being too absolute in their denials; and in the course of the book there are plenty of dogmatic statements. It is invigorating to find a pragmatist, who is bound to give soft answers, being so resolute in his claims that all values change, that ideologies depend entirely upon economic conditions, and that there is a historical process in which we can discern improvement. What is the criterion which enables him to be so sure about this? He takes for granted that man has now reached maturity and is entering into a new culture which will make past views outmoded. In describing historical change he relies far too much on Marxist theories about ideologies, how cultural and religious beliefs arise out of the economy of the period. He even goes so far as to give as evidence for this the various descriptions of God as Shepherd or King or Father. Shepherd is, let us agree, very natural in a pastoral society, but apart from this the relation of a shepherd to a flock will always suit as an image of God's providential care of man. As to King, it does not belong to any single one economic condition: it has proved universal, almost as universal as Father. So far as I know there has never been an economic condition in which human beings had no father or mother. It is surely very silly, not to say suicidal, to quote these images in favor of the Marxist explanation of varieties of religious experience. A much simpler explanation is that every race has chosen the best image it could find to describe the Maker of heaven and earth and Lord of all mankind. It would have been much wiser to look more closely at this supposed superstructure which varies with society's economic growth; it is surely a very wobbly one and can vary so much as to make the so-called uniformity only nominal.

Whatever the merits or demerits of Cox's treatment of change in history, he has no right to be so dogmatic in his statement of it. What perhaps is worse is that he has not realized the real problem in change, which he treats so cavalierly. Change of itself just means that one blessed thing after another happens. In evolution, however, and in development the problem is to what degree does the changing object keep its identity; how in fact identity and change can go together. Christianity has developed through the centuries, but, unless it has collapsed, there must be some identity between what it is now and what it was in the first century. If only Cox had fixed his mind on this, he would have written very differently about the Bible and its teaching, the early and medieval Church, and the connection today of Christianity with its past. What astonishes the reader are the careless assumptions, which belong to the genre of a gossip magazine. There is a problem worth serious study, for instance, in the so-called "relativity of morals." I have already pointed out how in the various civilizations in history the fundamental precepts of morality, as belonging to one family, the human race, keep appearing and reappearing. In the light of this agreement it is a fascinating study watching how the emphasis may change and one or another ethical ideal or prescript be overlooked; how again rules may appear to conflict as they do at the present day over birth control and war and authority's invasion on liberty. A mistaken idea of how human virility is passed on could cause the old to be put to death for the sake of the tribe's survival. Feudal landlords overstressed the offense of trespassing on land or stealing, not only to preserve their power but because land was their one insurance. Cox, however, accepts a passing theory put forward by Communists that morals are nothing more than a superstructure built over ephemeral economic conditions. Morals then are just an epiphenomenon and nothing more. What is not moral determines what is to be called moral for a time: the social position changes, the old is outmoded and disappears, and a new code of behavior comes into being, again determined by nonmoral factors. The only true conclusion to be drawn from such a theory is that morals have no more significance than the way one dresses or combs one's hair or chooses to walk down a street. In other words, here is a pure relativity of morals, which is a polite way of saying there are no standards at all. Dimly aware that he has taken up a very shaky position, Cox justifies himself by a bizarre manner of reasoning: "the relativization of values can have a much more constructive result, the recognition that since everyone's perspective is limited or conditioned, no one has the right to inflict his values on anyone else" (nor has anyone the right to question them). This thought might help a man who came last in a race at the Olympic Games, for he could console himself with the fancy that the winner was only relatively more successful. It would be less useful in a game of cards. When it comes to ethics, however, if there be any logic in his remark, the Nuremberg Trials were wrong for imposing our ideas of morality on the Nazis who were held for trial. The English missionaries to Fiji ought to have turned their eyes away when they came across cannibalism in 1835; nor should suttee have been suppressed by law in India. If once we accepted Cox's justification in matters of truth and falsehood, any lie or any untruth would become excusable. Oddly enough in the very sentence which I have quoted Cox lays down an absolute, saying "no one has the right . . ."

Equally dogmatic are other statements such as "that God is hidden—that he is, in fact, *ex officio* hidden." I am not clear what *ex officio* means when applied to God. That does not matter much because the next sentence ends the subject once and for all with a ringing dogma: "Hiddenness is intrinsic to his nature as God." This is only one instance chosen out of many dogmatic or metaphysical statements which Cox has to make in order to prove himself a relativist and antimetaphysician. Sometimes he even writes as a traditionalist Christian: "In the historic process itself man meets the One who calls him into being as a free deciding self . . ." This is just a paraphrase of "There is a living God who creates man as a free being." In presuming to call man a "free being" Cox is happily Christian, but I wonder how he proves this to be true from pragmatic principles?

Free will is an absolute. Man either has it or does not have it. God, also, by a Christian must be accepted unconditionally, whether by reason and faith or as some believe by faith alone. But in what he writes about God Cox moves as uncertainly as the scientists in their search for the "missing link" between man and his apelike ancestors. He prefers to say that God is alongside man in the teamwork which goes on in technopolis; but God plays second fiddle in the human orchestra, and indeed is a hidden presence in the modern forum and city hall. He will no longer be found in church or chapel, and it is left unclear whether God has an existence of his own outside the realm of man. How we are to name God and to think of him will emerge "in the tension between the history which has gone before us and the events which lie ahead." "Since," Cox continues, "naming is a human activity, embedded in a particular, sociocultural milieu, there is no holy language as such and the word 'God' is not sacred." To a St. Paul or a St. Augustine such language would have seemed blasphemous and its writer an idolater as making God out of our own image. But Cox does not intend this, for he adds, "presumably God will continue to live eons after English and all other languages have been totally forgotten." I do not know by whom they will be forgotten, but what he says is certainly true if naming God meant nothing more than calling God God or Deity or Yahweh or Divine Father. Unfortunately Cox means more than this, for in several places he says that man gives meaning to the world. This is part of pragmatic theory, and it is a cancerous part; and Cox is committed to it. He tells us, for instance, that "it is characteristic of urban and secular man that he perceives himself as the source of whatever significance the human enterprise holds. . . . Symbol systems, the constellations of meaning by which human life is given value and direction are seen as projections of a given society." He does not see that in so exaggerating a half-truth as to make man the creator of values, and of values dependent on the particular society in which he lives, he has done more damage to human life and dignity than the Deluge, which, in the Bible story, washed away all human traces except the Ark. This is the result of turning the personal equation into the Maker and Lord of truth. One result he does not appear to have noticed is that as knowledge is a "projection of society," God must be amongst the projections. So what is the point of appealing to the Bible and Bible history and to Christ as alongside man in his teamwork? It means nothing at all.

Once more there is a problem here about which Cox might have said something positive and illuminating, instead of showing himself so cramped and confined by the contemporary ideas and the society in which he is living. There is the problem of the human factor in knowledge, presented not only by the individual and his personal prejudices and historical limitations but also owing to the function of time in the development. Lastly, and this is the most important of all, human nature is handicapped. This is the problem which has vexed philosophers down the ages. Plato regarded human sensible experience as a "between" world, half real and half unreal. St. Thomas Aquinas distinguished between the concept and intuition. By concepts man reaches truth, but only slowly and by means of abstractions. Kant analyzed the make-up of man, and enlarged the subjective side, so that he used a language not too dissimilar from that of Cox. But he did not fall into the trap which awaited Cox. His answer has influenced all modern thought, though for my part I think that while he clarified the problem, his answer only heightened the difficulty. A writer of a book called *L'Action*, Maurice Blondel, has enabled many of the followers of Aristotle and St. Thomas to glimpse an answer hidden away in the old terminology. Intuition would now mean seeing the objective truth in its fullness and relationships—an alive truth which would go into the vibrant intuition of one's own self. Perfect self-knowledge and intuition of reality go together. But a concept is dead-sea fruit: it is static and limited, as Kant would say, from our being in time and space. We have an angular vision—an aspect and an abstraction which we hold on to because what we see in the object is relevant to our human condition at the time. Hence in every age there are new aspects, and the right procedure is to understand these as a further knowledge of objective reality: the wrong procedure is to surrender everything static, throw away objective truth, thereby emptying out the baby with the bathwater, talk airily of dynamic thought, pragmatism, and relativism, and end up having nothing of the real, permanent reality to possess and enjoy. This is the fate of pragmatists like Harvey Cox. Instead of being human they are left to be just voices, ventriloquists speaking through robots or computers.

The Secular City abounds in generalizations, some very suggestive, others far too hasty. For instance, how comes it that a scholar of his caliber can quote with approval the silly remark of Proudhon that the first Christians were secularists? Omitting the letters of St. Paul and the writings of St. John, we have the messages of St. Ignatius of Antioch which tell a very different story. Is it likely that the disciples of a crucified Lord living in expectation of his rapid return would have been men of this world? Again, he accepts the least meritorious idea of Bishop Robinson, his fuss about the damage done by the Greeks in introducing a spatial supernatural world. It was St. Paul, not a Greek, who talked of the third heaven and the seventh heaven. Bishop Robinson, though he is erratic on this matter of spatial images and on the harm they have done, remains within the bounds of credibility. But what can one think of the preposterous claim made by Cox that the Ascension of Christ as described in the beginning of the Acts represented the dislike of the early Christians for spatial images? "The Ascension in its simplest terms means that Jesus is mobile."

Almost as foolhardy a mistake is the assertion that these spatial static and pagan ideas endured in Christendom until the end of the eighteenth century, keeping priests and clergy immobile at home. "Only in the missionary movement of the nineteenth century and the ecumenical movements of the twentieth did the mistaken notions of Christendom begin to disappear." One might excuse his not knowing about the Nestorian missions which may have penetrated to China in the fourth and fifth centuries, the probable missions of an uncertain date to India with St. Thomas the legendary pioneer. He does not seem to realize that the conversion of France, England, Ireland, and the Rhineland, as well as of the Slavs, was due to missionary effort. The Franciscans made heroic journeys in the Middle Ages and were certainly "mobile," to use Cox's favorite word, as were the Crusaders. What is less excusable is his ignorance long before "the end of the eighteenth century" of the work of Francis Xavier, the apostle of the East; the extraordinary experiment of Robert de Nobili in becoming a Brahman; and the heroic rescue work among the Negro slaves of Peter Claver at Cartagena. But Harvey Cox is an American, and it is rather shocking that he has never heard of the superhuman work and the martyrdom of the French Jesuits, de Breboeuf, Isaac Jogues, and others in Canada and North America in the seventeenth century, and the work of the Franciscans in California.

Harvey Cox must have a far closer acquaintance with the Bible than he shows in his book. It is so disappointing that it is only brought in as evidence when it seems to lend some support to his predilections. He gives the impression that he thinks that Hebrew and Greek ideas are in striking contrast. It has become fashionable to emphasize this contrast, and to be silent about the part played by Greek ideas in, for example, the Sapiential books. St. Luke was a Gentile, and St. Paul was acquainted with Greek culture. St. Paul is free with his spatial categories in a way which ought to madden Cox, and when he talked about the heavens to which he had been raised his Jewish as well as his Greek converts would, I suppose, have understood him. One may ask, in fact, whether the Jews were not as fond of heights and spatial images as the Greeks. Did not Moses ascend Mount Sinai to converse with God, and perhaps thinking that thereby he would be nearer to God? The second letter of St. Peter refers with reverence to the "holy mountain" of the Transfiguration, and it is clear from the Gospels that Christ withdrew sometimes at night in order to spend hours with his Father in prayer on the hills or mountains. The most famous of all Christ's sermons is the Sermon on the Mount. The very name assures us of no distaste for spatial imagery, and it was in this sermon that the listeners were to pray to "Our Father who is in heaven," and later on in the prayer a distinction is made between earth and heaven.

Cox makes much of the earthly spirituality of the Jews,

and stretches this idea to include a special blessing on his technopolis. But whereas Cox spends all his time developing this city of the earth, this urban kingdom which Christ came to initiate, Christ himself is markedly silent on temporal and worldly blessings. His distinctive message begins with the Beatitudes and the Our Father. He will not allow the message of his Father to be misinterpreted and changed into a national or party cry. What belongs to Caesar give to Caesar, and what belongs to God must be rendered to God. Had the Sanhedrin found real evidence that Christ intended an earthly city—even as remarkable a one as Cox has in mind—they would have had a case against Christ. The claim shivers to pieces in the answer given to Pilate: "My kingdom is not of this world." It is clear that Pilate had a very different idea of Christ's intention from Harvey Cox's. No true description of the Gospel ideals and the kingdom of Christ can be given which does not put in the forefront the Cross, other-worldliness, and loving union with God himself. Paul preached no other doctrine than the Cross: "I preach Christ and him crucified, to the Jews a stumbling block, to the Gentiles folly, but to those who believe the power and the wisdom of God." In any attempt to reconcile Christianity with humanism this text must be reckoned with. There is too little divine folly in *The Secular City*. It has an altogether this-world kind of wisdom and accepts Christ only on its own terms. It makes God a confederate supporting a disinfected, smoothly run, rich-in-food, circus-enjoyable, material paradise.

I do not say that this is the whole story, and that the City of God and the City of Man necessarily stand in such opposition to each other as the Beatitudes and the Cross do to the secular city as outlined by Cox. There is another side to the Christian good news, which has come to the fore recently in a new understanding of certain passages in St. Paul of cosmic grandeur, in the tone of some of the decrees of the Second Ecumenical Council, and in the writings, for instance, of Teilhard de Chardin. It is a prayer of the liturgy, speaking of the dignity of human nature as created by God, which gives Christians encouragement to work with other minds of other beliefs to the making of a Christian humanism. But Harvey Cox seems to be uninterested in this kind of enterprise, and so he reduces mysterious texts, which open up vistas of eternity, to an improved version of a modern American city, the city as he describes it of "the switchboard and the cloverleaf." This for him is the same as that seen in vision by St. John in the Apocalypse, the feast of the Lamb, the eternal banquet rehearsed and partly realized in the Christian liturgy, the holocaust, the risen victim, and the nuptial songs and union. Cox tells us explicitly that "the biblical God is perceived in the whole of social reality, and Law and Gospel provide us an angle of vision by which we understand secular events including urbanization." The God of the Gospel is "the One who with freedom and responsibility points towards the future in hope." By the future, it is fair to say, he means the increase of temporal prosperity and leisure. The Law, on the other hand, includes "any cultural phenomenon which holds men in immaturity, in captivity to convention and tradition."

I am confident that if St. Paul were able to read this he would repeat the words he once uttered: *Non ita didici Christum*—"This is not the Christ I know," this is not what I learned from him. But perhaps the simplest comment on all such attempts to see in a modern secular city the incarnation of the Christian message is to be found in *The Times Literary Supplement* for March 23, 1967 p. 242): "All the strong effects of religion in the political sphere are indirect and generally undesigned. The religious men who have unwittingly changed the character of politics spent much of the day on their knees before God . . . Jean Paul wrote in 1809, 'Religion is not a Church parade of the State . . . heaven cannot become the lackey of earth, nor can the sanctuary be transformed into the State's cookshop.' "

CHAPTER 4

THE TWO
CITIES

When the dying Thoreau was
asked about immortality, he replied, "One world at a time."

"Prayer is the world in tune."

(HENRY VAUGHAN)

"Those things we call religious which are ordained to God as their
end. Those things we call secular which, though not religious, do not
envisage God as their end immediately. Thus a Church is called a religious building or an inn we call secular. But an inn is not therefore
irreligious. Those things are irreligious which are ordained to Mam-
mon as their end." (ERIC GILL, *Art Nonsense*)

As we have seen in the last chapter, the traditional belief
in the two cities or kingdoms, one of God, the other of
man, is now widely contested. Harvey Cox's *The Secular
City* is only one, though perhaps the most popular and
able, amongst many contemporary attempts to refute the
old dualism and present a Christian humanist city life. In
Cox's account the secular city swallows and digests to its
own good what is best in Christianity. Other writers do not
go so far as this, and their approach is somewhat different.
It is influenced by the new emphasis on history. In old days
truths were treated as tablets brought down from on high;
they defied time and space, being equally true and intelli-

gible in Persia or Peru, Rome or Peking, at the court of Akbar, Solomon, Constantine, or Charlemagne. Like good silver they might become tarnished, but they remained the precious metal which could be repolished.

This is what is now called the static view of history and repudiated by many philosophers and theologians, even amongst the more orthodox. The tendency now of these writers is to associate Christianity with the secular world by showing how Christian truth has constantly developed in and through the various cultures in which the Church has progressed. They therefore allow for a more definite contribution to society by religion than Harvey Cox, and as a consequence the features of Christian humanism become more distinct. Among the protagonists of this view are Karl Rahner, P. Michel de Cerveau, Michael Novak, and, to the surprise of some, both Fr. Bernard Lonergan, S.J., and the late Fr. John Courtney Murray, S.J. Fr. Lonergan has written in an article in *Focus 2* called *"Existenz und Aggiornamento,"* of a change from classicism to historical consciousness. An end has come to the culture of definitions, "the axis on which the whole human history turned for 2400 years." Socrates taught youth the necessity of defining, and replaced myth by definition. But now that kind of culture is over and done with. Aristotle sought certain knowledge of causal necessity, whereas now science deals with the probable and with verified possibilities. Our interest today is in the individual, the individual making choices for himself. But we do not yet know enough about our own myriad potentialities. Lonergan concludes that the crisis today is not a crisis of faith but of culture. But I should prefer to think that this crisis is due to the present relativism in our culture, which is far too easily considered as a permanent substitute for the older culture of definitions. Man as a consequence robbed of his certainties also feels robbed of his God and of his faith. What another well-known writer, Charles Davis, can make of a view such as that of Fr. Lonergan is shown in words which I have already quoted and criticized: "Classicism regards man as a nature already defined, essentially unchanging, and objective truth as fixed in unchanging concepts outside the mind. Historical consciousness sees man as a process or subject in a process of becoming. . . . Objective truth is a function of developing mind and is always marked by historicity." Fr. Courtney Murray, not long before his regretted death, expressed himself on this question of "static" truth and classicism. For him it was an outworn conception, standing in the way of progress and demanding certainties where we have no certainties. The classicist does not understand what is going on: "He doesn't understand the mentality behind it and the fact that this mentality, whether you like it or not, is at the moment the great dynamic historical force." To the classicist, truth is so objective that it can exist apart from anyone's possession of it with "ideas always up there in heaven." In such a view there is no such thing as a historical dimension to truth, no development, no growth. The cult of certainty is a product of classicism, but rather surprisingly Courtney Murray then goes on to call it a development especially of the Cartesian era. Nowadays we must realize that "truth is an affair of history and is affected by all the relativity of history. Truth is an affair of the human subject. Truth therefore is an affair of experience." We have to avoid the worship of certainties, for "if you bring certainty into question, you also bring authority into question," and a little later he goes on to say that "the theological way of putting the question today is not how certain we are. The question today is how much have we truly understood, how much more is there to be understood in the traditional affirmations to be related to my human interest and experience—their relevance."

On this matter of certainty I have already said something, and I shall return to it. For the moment I will point out that Fr. Courtney Murray is being quite revolutionary, for he belittles certainty as belonging to classicism. In the usual teaching on the nature of faith, Catholic theologians have stressed the reasonableness of it, laying less emphasis on experience both because it is so quicksilvery and because they thought the entrance to the faith must be by truth itself, informed by reason. Some years ago, let me say, in a book called *The Nature of Belief* I made a comparison between moral decisions and the act of faith. In moral decisions we are concerned with particular issues; what perhaps unfortunately Aristotelians called means to ends. Moral choices do fall within the concept of a good life. Must I tell the truth? Must I pay a man what he claims? Must I join up in a war or become a member of a particular party? At a certain moment very often the choice becomes so clear in the mind that one wonders how one could have hesitated. There is certainty—for doubts and difficulties have removed themselves or been removed. But now as compared with a moral decision, faith is a final decision of life or death, as Kierkegaard saw. We take our lives in our hands, but as against Kierkegaard I would say that the truth enlightens the mind, and Christ is seen as the way and as the truth and as the life. This is a certainty in which one's whole self is involved and one's attitude to life. This is why when bewildered with difficulties, not doubts, we cry out with St. Peter: "To whom shall we go, for Thou hast the words of eternal life?"

I say that this is a certainty of the first order, and I am not quite sure where Fr. Courtney Murray stands. He might to some extent agree, because he says that the Council Fathers rejected classicism and embraced "historical consciousness," for "they conceived the renewal of the Church to mean a turn to the sources of the life of the Church—the sources in history which are also transhistorical, the event of Christ and the Word of Christ in the Gospel." So in the final resort Courtney Murray, and others whom I may quote such as Louis Dupré, fall back upon a "trans-historical" or nonempirical ground for certainty and truth. But why associate "certainty" with a stick-in-the-mud attitude? This is a little hard to see, for certainty is an invaluable condition of mind if we are to keep our mental health, especially to one on the march and a voyager. Our minds should be made up, if we are to give of our best in any mission or enterprise, as, to take but one example, the visit of Judith to Holophernes shows. Hesitation is often fatal, and uncertainty blurs our vision; and as to our mental welfare, the couches of psychiatrists are filled with those who cannot have a rational confidence in themselves or their talents. What other intention had Lord Montgomery before Alamein than to create a confident belief and then a certainty among his troops that Rommel could be defeated and would be defeated? Furthermore one ought not to take an oath or make a vow or even promise or pass judgment unless one has moral certainty.

As one who has for a number of years now propagated similar views to those just mentioned, the witness of Michael Novak must be mentioned, especially as he has become a spokesman for many of the younger generation in America. He asks for a break with the theological habits and ideas which have kept on hardening since the Council of Trent. He is very free with words like "dynamic" and "historical," and by "historical" he means, first, that theologians should take notice that all the words they use have a history, and, secondly, that these words have been understood differently by different generations. Such an admonition on first reading sounds very important, for most of us do recognize that words can be misunderstood, and therefore we try to define the sense in which they are going to be used. A typical incident is one I remember of a lawyer pleading a case before a court of appeal. As a good Aristotelian he used the distinction of "formal" and "material"— where formal would come nearest to the word "essential."

Unfortunately for him, one of the judges understood "material" as relevant and "formal" as a matter of form. But, as I say, we can take care of our speech and our writing, or so we think. Novak perhaps legitimately exaggerates his case, because if the majority of words changed their meaning from one generation and one civilization to another, communication would become well-nigh impossible. So far from there being development, there would be a complete standstill. It looks then either as if the majority of words do not change or the substance of what is being taught remains practically the same. Novak is revolting against the idea that everything can be said once and for all at one time, and that there is nothing farther to do than repeat and repeat the same truth. Only a lover can do this with impunity. He is protesting against an immobile Church mumbling words which are no longer relevant. Time marches on and words undergo subtle changes. When King James II saw Wren's new St. Paul's in London he called it "amusing, aweful and artificial." Each of these words was then complimentary. But words by themselves are not enough; abstract definitions are not enough. Language is the plaything of human beings, their form of intercourse. "The efficacy of formulation . . . was to be judged by their success in the actual world, not by their coherence in a book or system." Theology when abstracted from history "seems to encourage intellectual duality; one has to think twice, once for theory and once for practice." Once again Novak is not bothering to be precise; he is on a theme close to his heart. The old-time theologian does "not seem to notice that languages change, that men's manner of understanding even the same sentences changes. . . . Men's point of view, experience, conceptions and language change. Men's grasp of truth, therefore, changes also." The static form of orthodoxy is a retreat from the responsibility of living in history and of remaining faithful to Christ under the stress of changing circumstances. This anti-

quated attitude saw "the Church as an anvil on which history rains its blows in vain: whereas the Church is also the
leaven in the loaf of history, a mustard tree or growing
vine." One must ask Novak why not use all these images?
The Gospels use many and as long as they are not flatly
contradictory they may serve to enlighten us on the
Church's mysterious and many-splendored beauty. Novak
gives the image of the vine, and that makes me think of
those lines which might serve as a text for him:

> Surely I have served thee as the wrinkled elm
> Yieldeth its vigour to the jocund vine.

But then the image of the vine, which the Fourth Gospel
tells us Christ used at the Last Supper, indicates such a
unity in the Church that it leaves little room for the kind
of change Novak wants. Christ is the vine and the members
of his loving creation the Church are as branches. If so,
there is an identity always wherever and whenever the
Church exists. Novak might retort that that is to take one
image too literally, and that may well be so, but there is a
certain uniformity in such images as those of the vine
branch, the leaven in the loaf, and the mustard tree. So
mysterious and unique, however, is the divine message,
that a multiplicity of images may well be necessary, even
the one of the anvil.

There is a saying of Poincaré's about the nature of scientific inspiration which may be apposite: "Ideas rose in
throngs: I felt them oppose one another until pairs inter-
locked, so to speak, making a stable combination." One
must add of course that the stable combination of the
Church is of "divine" workmanship that reconciles discord-
ant elements and makes them "cling together in one society." Novak and those who share with him a sense of the
importance of history in any estimate of Christianity and
its growth are strongly opposed to the old dualism, formu-

lated in the famous distinction of St. Augustine between the City of God and the City of Man. Most, I think, will welcome their attack upon what they call "angelism." By this they mean the attempt to deal with man as if he were a spirit mistakenly inhabiting a body. In past centuries the Gnostics bewailed the fact that the spirit was hampered by being enclosed in a body. The modern "angelists" are not philosophers. What they do is to make the ideal for man center in his spiritual activities. Man is not a composite being so much as a half-baked angel. This kind of thinking is endemic in the human race, for in most unexpected parts of the world there can be found a prejudice against the body and its functions. Plato made of this prejudice a sublime philosophy; and 'Christianity, partly because of the perennial prejudice and its early associations with Neoplatonism, can be all too easily presented by some of its followers as partially Gnostic or Platonic. Even St. Francis of Assisi confessed that he had treated Brother Ass too severely. The hermits and monks also probably helped to create an ascetic tradition in which the body had a very bad time. One mark still of the presence of this prejudice is the habit of speaking of Mind with a capital instead of the self or person and the personalizing of abstractions, such as Vitalism or Evolution, over and above the actual working of the body or of nature.

In advocating a Christianity inseparable from history, Michael Novak, P. Michel de Cerveau, Leslie Dewart, and many others stand for a Christian humanism of a sort. Christianity is not to be so closely identified with the secular world as Harvey Cox wishes, but the two should be inseparable. The secular city needs the virtues which Christianity preaches, and Christianity in its turn is invigorated by contact with the city, as the giant Antaeus drew strength whenever he touched the earth, Gaea, his mother. This theory clearly can admit variations. One, which Cox also drags in, is the Marxist: that religious ideologies arise out of economic conditions as a superstructure. P. Michel de Cerveau appears to be of this persuasion. In an article (*Concilium,* November 1966) called "Culture and Spiritual Experience," he contrasts spiritual writers who focus on the socio-cultural situation with those who look for the true expression of religious experience on the housetops away from all the noise of the marketplace and stock exchange. He regards the latter with disfavor as supporting the dualistic view mentioned above. In his opinion the shape and culture of each society has an important influence on the language in which religious ideals will be expressed. Modern writers, who have recognized the part which history plays in explaining the varieties of human life, tend therefore to hold that the form of spirituality is "something brought to the surface by the deep underground currents which give birth successively to the realms of ideas." Despite the mixed metaphors, there is unmistakable evidence for some kind of connection, though perhaps only of a simple and obvious kind. Lord (Bertrand) Russell tells us, for example, that as a child he was unusually prone to a sense of sin. "When asked what was my favourite hymn, I answered: 'Weary of earth and laden with my sin',"—an excellent example of the influence of English Victorian spirituality in the upbringing of children.

P. Michel de Cerveau is a strong partisan of the historical view. He is convinced that in each culture there is an implicit solidarity which makes all the forms of discourse and the interests in values fall within an implicitly accepted pattern. A certain set of truths is sure to comprise the assumptions from which new discoveries are made. They will be unquestioned, and they will form a pool of common interests. Hence "experience is always defined in cultural terms," whether it be literary or religious or political. What we behold is adaptation and adjustment and reformation constantly at work. As a consequence it is a wise tip to search for the special problems, difficulties, and adversaries in each age, for the representative ideas will be pointed and colored by the response to them. Those in the fray are unaware of this: each thinks that his views are above the merely popular battlecries and that they possess a timeless quality. So it is that a "culture" gives itself away in the spiritual movements strewn along its history: they represent its problems "thrown up in the course of evolution, its stresses etc. which explode in great drives."

There is obviously great force in this argument, for it does throw light on the past. But is it not too sweeping and also over-simple? Of course problems are framed and answered according to the needs and cultural propensities of an age. Yet certain discussions do seem to me to have a timeless air. Leaving out the stories, parables, and teaching in the Gospels as being divinely inspired and so *hors de combat,* the questions debated by Socrates do still have relevance, as do the sermons of John Chrysostom or John Donne, the ideas of Montaigne or Vico, the political views of Montesquieu and Abraham Lincoln, the mental discipline of Zen Buddhism. These are cases chosen at random. Again, though obviously they have a historical context, the issues over which St. Bernard and Abelard, Thomas More and Henry VIII, Galileo and the Holy Office, and finally Newman and Kingsley fought, have precisely their great value in that they transcended their particular times and cultures. What, too, of the rebels who fight against the dominant ideology of their time and come to be appreciated long after, men born out of due time, prophets who were sometimes stoned to death? The examples to prove his thesis which de Cerveau gives are somewhat disappointing. He cites the Crusades as "a political sublimation and expression of vital collective need." This is irritatingly vague. Then the approval of spiritual poverty is said to belong to a time when all ties were being loosened and the foundations of security shaken. In the sixteenth century the rise of the Illuminati is attributed to the changeover from angelology and cosmology to a religious psychology gravely affected by disenchantment with long-enjoyed religious traditions. Similar explanations are sprung on the reader touching changes in the eighteenth century and the problems connected with the end of colonialism. The spiritual language at each of these episodes, we are told, betrays the changes going on in society; but why should it not? In the same fashion he would explain how and why we have become familiarized with the spiritual language of today, which differs so markedly from the past, a language in which culpability, confession, conscience, teamwork, dialogue, and a communion liturgy have become household words.

P. de Cerveau says that we are committed to his view if we want to avoid that solecism of affirming an essential core in experience with an unchanging vocabulary all its own. Both history and sociology rule this out, for it is fatal to look outside experience for explanations and for nonempirical objects. Man's yearnings in cultural situations always take flesh. "It is through this medium that he finds God, yet ever seeks Him, that he expresses his faith, that he carries on simultaneous experiments in colloquy with God and with his actual brothers."

In this defense of his view P. de Cerveau seems to disregard the possibility that experience itself may demand a nonempirical factor or core, as is the case with our own human nature. Even in living organisms there is a structure which remains recognizably the same while it is changing. I have already suggested that the problem of development has not really been faced. Furthermore, in the last quotation from P. de Cerveau he would appear by using the word "simultaneous" to rule out any colloquy with God separate from that with his brothers. That does not prevent him from taking for granted that our human experience contains and expresses a desire for union with God. This having been posited, he goes on to say that we find the language for this experience and implicit dialogue with God in the ever-changing situations encountered in history. He then tries to show how this happens. In the sixteenth and seventeenth centuries Europe broke up into nations with their own religious and political structures, but these were so unstable that they led to peasant revolts and famines. Meantime a new idea was emerging, namely, that of nature as a force sweeping all before it, and this had its repercussions in the religious atmosphere. Man began to think of himself as a traveler, no longer astray in the world, but rather as one *led* astray in the world. He no longer expected to find traces of God in the world. Instead he looked for order and certainty in himself and in his own ideas. Berkeley, Spinoza, and Hegel are intelligible only in this context. De Cerveau pushes this cultural spiritual change even further, for he sees growing out of it a literature of illusion. Writers begin to describe the world as a bubble without substance, as an appearance without any background. Then, following on their skepticism about the external universe, they look with favor on mystical ideas of a world within. De Cerveau thinks it striking and suggestive that St. Teresa called this interior world an "Interior Castle." Certainty now is sought within; man discovers in himself what transcends self, and so becomes more certain of the reality of God. Unexpectedly this new certainty is said to lose its individualistic flavor and embrace humanity. A new interest develops in the making of a right social order, and liberty, equality, and fraternity appear on the horizon.

Perhaps some may find it difficult to see the necessity which links together these various historical phases and the religious reaction. P. de Cerveau, however, is sure that they exist, and he then proceeds to explain how the present religious crisis too is a reflection on the changes in history. More and more is the word "experience" used in religious literature. This experience is largely responsible for the changing attitude to religion, for we are told it leads to high expectations of meeting God, and the result is a vacuum. "Today as yesterday and for ever we visit the place where Christ should be lying and find an empty tomb." Our language proves pitifully inadequate, and so we seek for a new language. The Christian would live on the evangelical truths and on tradition, but they move away into the distance, and the language is dead. Hence he feels in the wilderness and not at home in the new language which is being forced upon him. What is worse, he is made more and more aware of the break between what he is preaching and what he and others are doing outside the performance of religious duties. It is at this point that P. de Cerveau brings us back to the problem of the two cities and of humanism, after what may have looked like wandering afield. Man now can hear only his own voice when he addresses God. He relies on faith that there is Someone speaking, and he comes to realize that God is revealing Himself as that without which or whom life is impossible. Life therefore here and now must not be sought in some rare out-of-this-world experience: it is rooted in history and in society and especially in the Church. As for theological language, it would not do to reject it altogether, even though the Presence, spoken of prophetically and liturgically, cannot be immediately grasped or understood in the terms of any particular language. In fact language, symbols, the best of experience, all display a defectiveness and bring to light something different which would improve the word or the experience were it present. Hence we can never identify the Presence in any one experience or hold eternity in an hour or perfection in our clumsy hands. Therefore de Cerveau tells us that the theology of experience can only be a theology of distance. Truth can only be expressed in terms resonant with history and such an expression is bound to be relative.

If this be so, it is an error to hold on to a single truth as the one and only sign and symbol of salvation. De Cerveau calls such practice "fixation," namely, taking a passing phase as the whole truth. It shows we have not realized that every genuine experience contains likeness and unlikeness and points to a higher union in the midst of differences. Truth emerges in a dialogue, where there is reciprocity and a recognition that the opposing view has something to support it. It is the Devil who comes down on the side of the *status quo*. The saint who gathers disciples imparts to them his ideas; but he realizes the interior paradox belonging to what is only one, and that a special form of fidelity to the Infinite.[1] It is his followers who turn what was a movement, an expression of love, into an object, an ideology, and stand for the letter of the law. They fail to see that such truths are in a movement and that they carry with them an expectation of something still to be said, which will disclose still more of the Infinite. This is why history

[1] I think P. de Cerveau is wrong in saying that the saint realizes that his plan or intention does not contain an absolute in it. The saint, like a great mathematician, is struck all of a heap by the truth which has come to him from on high, and sees the work he plans as God's very plan. He has that kind of inexorable certainty where beauty and truth meet—one so well described by Bertrand Russell in his discovery of Euclidean geometry at the age of eleven: "This was one of the greatest events of my life, as dazzling as first love. I had not imagined there was anything so delicious in the world." Martin Thornton adds a further thought. He holds that a special kind of certainty is reached by the saint owing to his habitual recollection, which is a precursor of the gifts of the Holy Spirit. He is thereby enabled to know deep things and truths without metaphysics or prolonged reading in theology. "He judged the cause of the poor and the needy: then it was well with him; was not this to know me? saith the Lord." Such knowledge can be rightly called "static," if the time element be ignored in static truths. How little time counts is shown in the apparently contradictory experience of two mystics—the Rip Van Winkle who thought he had been away only a few minutes or hours and found a score of years or more had passed, and the mystic who at the moment of ecstasy knocked over his pitcher of water. Coming to, he felt an eternity had passed, but the water had not yet ceased pouring from the overturned pitcher.

has shown so many good ideas, so many movements that are catalysts of the past, and then they themselves have to be renovated or changed.

This account contains so much that is good that I am reluctant to criticize it: it gives, I believe, the beginning of an answer to one at any rate troubling problem. It is this, that for all its apparent finality truth does not stand still— and no generation just repeats what the preceding one taught as true. It may be called the inconstancy of the human mind (how like a busy bee it is!), but should we not thank God that we have not in every age to say the same thing, in the same words? Let there be always certain sacred, not-to-be-touched truths, but even they like a diamond can look differently and show new facets in different lights. Providence has so arranged that every generation can think it has spoken the last word, even as beaters of the world's records in athletics, or the makers of poems like Goethe, or musicians like Beethoven, are thought to have reached the limit of perfection in their arts. P. Michel de Cerveau does help us to understand how this can happen, but while he brings out the nature of the problem so defiantly, I think he has omitted some considerations adverse to his view. Hence it falls short of finality itself. He is obviously one with Michael Novak and others in claiming that truth must always be looked for in its historical setting. A dynamic point of view must prevail against the static, and it is important for humanism that it should do so: otherwise we would have to rely on very dusty answers and be content with going for information about Christianity to some old papyrus.

An interesting variant on this type of view has created a stir in university circles. It is *The Future of Belief* by Leslie Dewart. In his book he argues that the theology of the Christian faith needs drastic changes if it is to keep abreast of our contemporary culture. All faiths must follow this line or die. Therefore, most of the old stage properties must be thrown away, as stone weapons yielded to bronze and bronze to steel. The chief encumbrance from the past is Greek thought. The early Church looked to Greek ideas wherewith to clothe the words of salvation. Helpful as these ideas may have been then, they have been responsible for an outstanding weakness in Christian theology and philosophy. The Greeks had no sense of the function of time in the growth of ideas: they sprung, full grown, like Athene from the head of Zeus. Hence the Church was left with a set of principles and doctrines becalmed while the world sailed on. Dewart, however, is not merely a critic. He proposes a new language and a new philosophy, which he believes relevant to the world we now live in.

Dewart is courageous and as adventurous as Teilhard de Chardin. To overthrow all the categories, the tablets of the law, consecrated by Augustine, Aquinas, and so many pontiffs, invites hostile criticism. He concentrates his batteries especially on the traditional Scholastic theory of knowledge. According to this theory, truth consisted in the conformity of the mind with what is perceived in the real world. These are intelligible objects, in fact all that is existing is by its very nature intelligible, even though much has yet to be grasped and learned, and much may surpass the power of the human mind. When the intelligible object becomes known for what it is, it is judged to be a true idea of the mind, conforming with the existent object. St. Thomas takes over the brilliant discovery of Aristotle that an object when actually known is identical with the actual conceiving of it—that is, the concept—except in the way they each exist. The real object exists out there in the world; as an idea or concept it exists in the mind; otherwise they are identical when we think truly. Now Dewart will have none of this, and he gives us an alternative which he believes shows the dynamism in thinking. Truth, he tells us, "as the property of human conscious experience is not tied down to the substantial stability of concepts. Truth does not depend upon the conformity of experience to reality. Rather it should depend upon the realization (that is, the actual coming-to-being) of human experience precisely as human experience; that is, of consciousness, as consciousness differentiates itself from the world (that is, relates itself to itself and to an-other.)" He then calls his version of truth "Man's self-achievement within the requirements of a given situation." Adequation to reality, which is one of the words he retains from the old terminology, "connotes adjustment, usefulness, expediency, proficiency, sufficiency and adaptation."

Now unless we already knew what truth was, I doubt if we could make head or tail of this description, certainly not derive our notion of truth from it; and this looks like a flaw in Dewart's explanation. What he says might serve as an interesting sidelight on truth, or present us with a new aspect which had been neglected. What appears original is the stress laid on the personal appreciation of truth, how it ingrows and makes for our own self-realization. But this is not as new as he supposes. The school of P. Rousselot, A. Valensin, and Maréchal noted and made much of this double role of knowledge—the grasp of the real and the perfecting of the self. This school was not much to the liking of Maritain and Gilson, which may be the reason why Dewart, as a pupil of these Thomist masters, ignores it. He would have benefited by consulting Rousselot, for example, for in his own version the weak spot is the criterion of truth. He grounds truth in consciousness being of its very nature social and cultural. But cultures differ, and sometimes a people can become dulled by convention or intoxicated by drugs, as happened to some savage tribes; or so biased by a sense of futility and misery, as in Buddhism, or so inflamed by power, as in Nazism, that the culture stands in the way of truth and self-realization instead of catering to them. There would be no chance of conceptualizing the truth, to use Dewart's phrase, in such circumstances. Nevertheless the individual genius and the cultural background do pass into each other quite often enough to justify a mitigated version of Dewart's view, and it can be richly illustrated. But examples are more easily chosen from the arts than from intellectual works. E. M. Gombrich, for instance, has brought out how intimately the landscapes of Constable are a spiritual extension of childhood love for the mill on the banks of the Stour. Even more illuminating perhaps is that painting by Botticelli of *The Adoration of the Magi,* where the unchanging mystery of the Incarnation turns our attention to Florence and young worshippers gathered in Florentine dress, and Botticelli himself turns to face us and make us all one despite distance of time and place. Dewart's view then can be well illustrated in the arts; but in the study of history it is less convincing, for most are agreed that an adequate account of a period or great event cannot be given by those contemporary with it. Time must pass before such events are seen in their proper perspective. Even less tied to the moment than the historian is the philosopher, who must pick his words and so state a problem that the answer stands beyond the caprice of time.

Rousselot, as I have said, combines the grasp of reality and the heightening of self-knowledge, but whereas Dewart tells us that the problem of knowledge has its answer in the process of self-differentiation or self-realization, Rousselot remains intent on looking at the objective world. Knowledge is first and foremost a true judgment on the nature of reality, and for that judgment objective evidence must be sought. On this simple truth heaven and earth, and all that is, hang together. At the same time Rousselot assures us that our knowledge would be, though exact in detail, lifeless and without aim were it not directed both to the divine and to the good of the self. Thus he writes:

One can regain in the throbbing dualism, which characterises the first apprehension (of the mind), the distinct trace of the two loves which draw the soul along: in so far as it translates the sensible given into a something, into essence, the soul desires itself, it wishes to realise itself as humanity; in so far as it affirms that being exists it wishes to realise itself as being, it desires God. But these two loves are not external to one another; the love of God, as St. Thomas explains, is internal to the love of self: it is its soul. Furthermore, it is the first source of our intellectual light; if the soul is sympathetic to being, as such, it is finally because it is capable of God. (*Revue de Philosophie,* March 1910, translated by Ralph Harper.)

Rousselot here hammers out a theory which embraces two loves, what I, in another place, have designated Eros and Agapé, one where love in all we do seeks the good of the self, the other is on an existential plane and looks beyond itself and sees a reality to which it must conform. By the cooperation of the two we perfect our humanity and so are the champions of the one genuine humanism. A modern empiricist might raise his eyebrows at this confident metaphysical approach, but Dewart is well trained in metaphysics and should not be discomforted by it. Rousselot allows for what Dewart calls "the conceptualisation of a growing self-consciousness." Moreover he is prepared to admit the defects of conceptual thinking, its abstract nature, its dependence on sense, its apparent static character. But it is a bridge over to the objective world, and one does not burn one's bridges. Without it we lose contact with the world outside us, and can have no certainty of the truth of our statements. To appeal to the heightening or intensification of consciousness will not serve. Our own fancied enhancement (the image of LSD and mescaline occurs here) will not ensure by itself contact with reality; we need a bridge. This criticism is a general one applicable to all forms of knowing. Dewart made his innovation a general one, one which would replace the old theory of the mind's conformity with the real. But of course this same defect that I have tried to point out in his view will prove even more serious in the matter of the Christian faith. Here the intensification of consciousness will not do at all. If Christianity be true, we have to get out beyond our own experience, however high and noble. It is to God speaking that we must listen, and hear authentic news from God Himself touching our worship of Him, our sacrifice of ourselves, and, in the old sense of the word, our atonement with the divine nature. Owing to reliance on human experience, man has too often been deceived. We have had enough bad copies of masterpieces in art, reproductions of Greek sculpture, of a Donatello or a Giorgione or a Rembrandt, to put us on our guard. If this be so of man's work, how much more sedulous should we be to ascertain with objective certainty where the devine message is to be found, the message which St. Peter recognized in the words, "To whom shall we go? Thou hast the words of eternal life."

When this has been said and accepted, it is fair to add that there is no essential relation between a theology which depends on Greek philosophical ideas and divine faith. Theoretically there may be several other systems which could carry and articulate the Creed. Not only that: we are not even necessarily tied down to any special or exclusive theory of truth. Experience here has much to say, and Dewart's insistence on the notion of "presence" may well come to be accepted as a latent truth which has finally come to the fore. "Presence" is that which is so distinctive in self-consciousness. To Dewart it is the decisive feature that separates a human being from an animal. "The point is," he writes, "that in the very act of knowing an object (whether a being other than himself or the very being which is himself) he becomes present to himself. . . . From the outset of consciousness he is always present to his own being." "Sum or sursum is the original fundamental human experience." From another angle phenomenologists like Husserl, and especially Merleau-Ponty, have shown how through the body the world outside us is present to us from the start. It does more than what is called "conaesthesia," that is, the sense we have of being embodied, that awareness which is always with us though we may seldom reflect upon it; but the body also makes present to us the reality around us, so that we are not startled by contacts—we stretch out our hands and legs confidently and with the greatest rapidity gain a knowledge of the third dimension and perspective.

In other words, we start with a world; we do not have to invent it or prove it. In a preceding chapter I suggested that as the body makes us, so to speak, one of its trade unionists from the beginning, so on a higher plane our spirit adapts itself to a world which reaches out immaterially and is thronged with objects like ourselves: we and they have familiar intercourse with truths and ethical standards and possibilities of loveliness. Dominating this world as the Absolute of absolutes, the ultimate love which makes human loves meaningful and ever stimulates men and women in every generation to scientific pursuits, is the idea and reality of God; One who as Alpha presides at the beginning, and as Omega closes the book of life at the end. To Dewart, God is best described in terms of presence, thereby corroborating the suggestion I have just made of a plane of existence or spiritual world which is our natural climate. God, he tells us, is a presence which "reveals me to myself in a supererogatory and gratuitous way, that is, by making me 'more fully myself' than I should be if I were not exposed to its impact." He regards this as the only valid proof for the existence of God (a "proof" not very likely to convince a rationalist). He would have it that only the language of "presence" and "absence" fits talk about God. To some, let me say, this sounds as if God were answering to a roll call; on the other hand, this language is to be found in such distinguished philosophers as Heidegger and Jaspers, and it has this advantage, that it disposes of false images and false concepts of God and does hint at the special relationship which must exist between the soul and God.

Dewart has a prejudice against so-called truths which appear to him to be static. He states that "the notion of the stability of truth leads to its annihilation." In this, as we have seen, he is at one with many contemporary Christian writers and humanists. He, however, gives a special twist to this modern view and makes it more philosophic. Knowledge is not a flat reproduction of the real world; we grow by continual, fresh conceptualizations, based on the growth of self-consciousness. All real knowledge promotes farther knowledge, a more intensified self-consciousness. The naïve idea that reality lies open before us, wholly intelligible and waiting to be discovered, must be abandoned. He quotes Wittgenstein in support of his contention that language cannot be understood as "a set of pointers or signs which indicate their corresponding concepts." (It will be noticed that this is nearer to Locke than Aristotle, and also a kind of retraction by Wittgenstein of an earlier simple correspondence view of knowledge.) All our ideas are cultured or social forms, and in no way are they made up by individuals finding names for specific objects and constructing conceptual lexicons. But the argument does not, I think, lead to the massacre of these innocent concepts. All now know that languages are cultural forms to this extent at least that a child learns a way of communicating which belongs to the ethnic group in which it was born. That does not prevent the same person, when he or she has matured, from asking about the meaning of terms, what they represent or point to. The educated person now has several languages at his disposal, and he can compare the Latin and the Greek of roughly two thousand years ago with the modern use of a word in English, French, and Spanish. He will notice the nuances of each ethnic group and see also the identity persisting which allows him to read the *Agamemnon*, the *Georgics, Don Quixote,* Ruskin, Proust, and Ezra Pound without qualms. Moreover concepts are indeed necessary for communication, but truth resides in the judgment when a man knows what he is doing and what the concepts can tell him. Surely Dewart and other contemporary writers and nominalists are exaggerating the relativity of our contacts with the real world by overstressing cultural and social differences. Take the inscription which a Bishop Abercius, aged seventy-two, made for his tomb while still alive in A.D. 216. I take this example because it bears on the question of development in doctrine and illustrates the foreignness of the Credal language which nevertheless is so easily understood. The latter part of it runs: "Faith led me everywhere forward, and everywhere provided me my food, a fish of exceeding great size and perfect, which a holy Virgin drew with her hands from a fountain: and this faith ever gives its friends to eat, it having wine of great virtue and giving it mingled with bread." It does not need a scholar to read and understand this language about the fish, with its Greek letters spelling out Jesus Christ Son of God, Savior, and the Virgin birth and the Eucharist. Instead of ethnic differences darkening the abiding truths, they tend, as here in this text, to enlighten us. The past is not separated from us to any substantial degree, and I do not think that any writer worth his salt writes just for the present. I have made a monument stronger than brass, said the Roman poet; and Pericles, if we can trust Thucydides, spoke to the Athenians with pride that their achievement would last for ever. Socrates, stirred by conscience and the words of the oracle, sought passionately for truth and justice, and would have been scandalized if he had been told that what he was saying was relevant only to his own time. We do not read Plato's dialogues just with an antiquarian interest. They have in fact helped to form our Western culture, and we read them still in order to learn and to take part in a dialogue in which men of all ages can join, a dialogue which is sufficiently independent of time to allow all to participate. This is a more mellow continuity than that of Dewart's where every generation is sitting uncomfortably on the shoulders of its predecessor and consigning its precepts and concepts to the dustheap.

A humanism which lives for the present and thinks of the past in terms of hieroglyphics is no more than a torso. This may seem very unfair to a Leslie Dewart, and perchance it is, for he has a panacea, namely, history itself. History for him is man living, thinking, and creating, and he accuses the old theorists of ignoring this outstanding characteristic of human nature, and specifically human consciousness. He is quite radical and stops at nothing. He maintains that even our idea of God must change. "To think of him [God] as existing in a simultaneous duration above time is to force the Christian faith into a hellenic mould which is not large enough to contain it." And again: "What Christians may realise better in the future is that as man's consciousness develops, we must conceive God as historical or *not at all.*" It may well be true that Christian theologians have neglected to their detriment the importance of the factor of time and history, but Dewart's remedy is so drastic that it looks as if in pulling down the pillars of the old temple, like Samson he has brought about his own death; for his own theory must be just as relative as those of the past, which are now over and done with. His chief charge against the past is, as we have seen, that it relied on a false view of the correspondence of concepts with real objects. It was a philosophy of static, full-sized objects which always kept their status. It assumed that we knew what species and genera were, and what belonged to them, and so we still ticket objects by their specific names and natures.

How far this bill of indictment is fair it is difficult to say. Science certainly has grown very modest in its claims. Both St. Thomas Aquinas and a modern scientist talk about appearances. The latter uses mathematical physical methods and distinguishes objects by observing how they work and by experimenting with them. He might while resting at night indulge in a theory that all physical, and perhaps even psychical, movements are variations of one force or energy, kinetic and radioactive, but in his laboratory he is concerned only with the appearances which his instruments allow him to observe. They are his yardstick. The word "appearances" has a more limited meaning for the scientist than for a philosopher like St. Thomas. To St. Thomas an appearance is the appearance of an object, how it appears, and not something assumed to have a reality of its own. But even to St. Thomas's mind there is a severe limitation imposed upon our knowing because of our dependence on the senses, the slow way we have to form ideas, and the absence of intuition. We have, so to speak, to keep walking around any object we see in order to have an adequate—and not even then perfect—knowledge of it. There is no need to elaborate on all the difficulties and limitations we encounter in learning. Everyone finds them out for himself, the varying power of memory and imagination, the deceptions of the senses, the abstractions we end up with instead of a vibrant apprehension of something individual and unique. So we might well agree up to a point with Dewart's criticism. Our knowledge tends toward the static and the abstract, as bread tends to get stale, and our knowledge is very seldom if ever an exhaustive grasp of the object we think about or contemplate. But all this is like a twice-told tale. Kant in his *Critiques* made it common property. He so limited human knowledge that it was judged incapable of proceeding beyond the phenomenal world. The human mind is an apparatus capable of making order by means of space and time in what is presented to it by the senses. Without the senses it bombinates *in vacuo*. Thus he blanked out all metaphysical knowledge and all conceptual knowledge about God or the spiritual world. In allowing no breakthrough, except by postulates, his critics say that he robbed himself of the right to say the things he did, and, as always, when one expels nature it creeps in again. I doubt if any empiricist can get on without implying more than he has allowed himself. He behaves like the child who said that God sat down on a chair and then created the world. It is for this reason amongst others that I have suggested above that man lives on two planes or in two climates, the one given to him by his body, the other by his spirit. But the trouble is that in this latter world of noumena he is without the tools to do a perfect job there. He does have real knowledge, but it is the kind which Dewart and so many others repudiate. They are ashamed of their birthright.

The limitations of human knowledge are threefold—a natural one, a cultural equation, and a personal equation —and the disservice they do can be recognized without recourse to any *a priori* or Kantian type of theory or to Dewart's alternative. The personal equation is always with us, just as one man makes more noise than another in all he does, or fidgets or rubs his nose, or rushes his fences, or cannot take a difficulty of an adversary seriously. Every historian has a personal equation, which is not so pronounced as a bias though it can pass into one. Sometimes it adds to the interest of a book or an opinion; at other times, like love, it can both aid the eye to pick out what is hidden, and also blind one. Cultural equations are similar, but on a larger scale, as the French and English differ on the matter of wit and humor. The well-known history of the love affairs of the elephant by a Frenchman, a German, an Englishman, and a Spaniard, which is meant as a satire on their respective cultures, tells us much briefly about this cultural equation. Neither it nor the personal equation drive us into Dewart's camp. We are left then with the limitation due to our very nature and the way we think. Dewart would have us free ourselves from this limitation with its static objects and abstractions by discarding the correspondence or conformity-with-the-object theory of knowledge and concentrating on the intensification of self-consciousness. I have already agreed that there is or can be an intimate connection between knowledge of reality and knowledge of the self in the form of a heightening of our conscious life. That is true, but only on a condition which Dewart has rejected, the condition that we verify our ideas by seeing that they correspond with the facts or events. Dewart's view resembles a man in a balloon who as it rises begins to go blind. No matter how exhilarated he becomes in mind or body, or ingenious, or heroic, he will never know whether he is going in the right direction or still rising. All depends on whether he is able to see the earth which he has left. Static knowledge as well as dynamic knowledge is needed, and Leslie Dewart has as much need as Harvey Cox to ponder over the Pauline text about being "steadfast and immoveable." In truth the famous lines by Roy Campbell criticizing some, as he thought, posturing and mindless poets are relevant here:

> They praise the firm restrain with which you write;
> I'm with you there of course.
> You use the snaffle and the curb all right,
> But where's the bloody horse?

The question of the general relativity of truth, and, following on that, of the relative merits of static and dynamic truths, has not yet been fully answered. The longstanding distinction between absolute and relative certainties still seems to be the most practical, but it has to be clarified. Relative certainties may look like nonsense, a contradiction in terms, but this rests on an older division of truth into metaphysical or logical truth—with which mathematics would be conjoined—physical certainty and moral certainty. The first gives us the kind of knowledge which we see it is impossible to deny. We see *why* what we are saying must be true. The second lacks this kind of certainty because the possibility of the case being otherwise is not ruled out. Nevertheless we would rightly be thought out of our mind if we questioned some certainties outside the schoolroom. The public does accept without hesitation the fruits of practical science as they are shown in innumerable products. All day long from the time we get up from a bed, stand on a floor, turn on the water, move about the house, trust staircases and doors and the sidewalk and what we eat and what we buy, we are exhibiting this second kind of confident certainty. Scientists also do the same, for they cannot possibly themselves test by immediate experience and experiment all the information they are constantly receiving. Even if they could they would still grant, I think, that the toast at breakfast will not walk off the table or the dish run away with the spoon. They do not expect to get nourishment from eating nails or knives, or hear the same tune if they play a score backwards. They do not copy Macbeth and ask themselves in serious doubt: Is this a dagger or perhaps a Nobel prize I see before me? What a strange world we would be living in if we could not take for granted innumerable facts and details of an everyday life! Imagine what X would think if on returning from Jerusalem his friend Y spoiled his story by saying he did not really believe there was such a place as Jerusalem because he had never been there.

This last example brings one to the third kind of relative certainty, which once was called moral certainty. This is a misnomer or at any rate ambiguous as it covers different subject matters. Our knowledge of the past is a "moral" certainty, for we have no doubt about many facts of which we can have no direct experience. Similarly, as in the instance of Jerusalem, there are many places on a map which we have never seen. Ancient cities, too, of which there are remains visible or dug up. Can we be said to have certainty that there was a city of Troy, that its locality has been discovered, and that there is a high probability—and nothing more?—that there were seven cities? But the ambiguity comes from the use of this adjective "moral" in a single, specific sense derived from the subject matter, namely, morals or ethics. Positivist philosophers have been very reluctant to allow that the distinction of true and false is applicable to morals. The reason they give is that morals are concerned with values and not with matters of fact. Nevertheless here again, if we consult world opinion from time immemorial—*securus judicat orbis terrarum*—there is an overwhelming verdict in favor of there being certainties concerning conduct, a certainty that honesty and mercy are good and fraud and hardheartedness wrong. To prove the correctness of general opinion we have to fall back on an ontological argument. In all living things there are actions and pressures which are good for the life of the plant or animal, actions and pressures which are adverse. One sort help to perfect, the other to subvert life. The same holds true with man, with a difference, a difference which arises owing to what I have claimed is his existence in a climate analogous to that of the body but higher. In this climate utility passes over into intrinsic values. Not only does an action benefit the life of a man and mankind, but it has a grace of its own which makes it beautiful and morally good. Furthermore—and this provides further evidence for the existence of God, and of a City of God over and above the secular city—an act which is advantageous or disadvantageous to the self and society takes on the character of a categorical imperative. Conscience is made aware of actions which are absolutely forbidden and of duties, which again are absolute and must be performed. Here then is the ground of our certainties in morals, as in other spheres of life. There is, therefore, no valid reason for removing certainties and absolutes and replacing them by pragmatic criteria, which will vary in different cultures, even as ideologies do. But if this be so, then Harvey Cox and de Cerveau and Leslie Dewart have been too hasty in denouncing static truths. There must be a way of reconciliation between what is static and dynamic, between being and becoming, the fixity of doctrine and its power to evolve. Various possibilities suggest themselves. If we look at nature there are all sorts of surprises, even puzzles, to the mind of a child. That the egg it eats at breakfast might have become the chicken served at dinner, that the grubby caterpillar should turn into the graceful and delicate butterfly, pass comprehension. Not so incomprehensible but nevertheless surprising is to see first a peahen and then a peacock, and finally to watch the expanding of the wondrous tail. If there be such changes as this in nature within one species and one family, might there not be equally astonishing facets of a truth revealed by time? Suppose that we treat knowledge as a kind of map, a *mappa mundi,* which is round and accurate. Its accuracy means that whatever we discover must conform with the world as represented by the map; but this granted, what an enormous number of discoveries will be made as we learn more and more about the real world! Like to this image of a map is that of a circle which from being bare can become full. Karl Rahner has said that a dogmatic definition of the Church is not an end but a beginning. This statement, if understood superficially, is, as I have already pointed out, surely defective. Because if there be a continuity and development, then there is something whose identity continues in the development, and therefore to imply that there is no end, that is, nothing final and complete, is to make shipwreck both of the dogma and development. What Rahner must mean is that a divine truth is an incitement and a way to the closest immediacy of communion with God. To his mind the reason why a formula is always being transcended is not just because of the kind of mind we have, which has to grow in wisdom, nor because of faith, which transforms the propositional forms into a movement of the mind to God's self as truth. It is due to the formula itself. All human statements, even those in which faith expresses God's saving truths, are finite; that is, they never declare the whole of a reality. In the last resort every reality, even the most limited, is connected with and related to every other reality. Therefore the propositions of faith are never adequate. But to be inadequate is not to be false, and moreover a true statement opens "prospects as to facts, realities, truths, which had not been seen explicitly in the earlier formulation, and which make it possible to see the same reality from a new point of view, in a fresh perspective." Here is a change, but not of identity, and "nothing need be given up."

Rahner in these last two sentences carries on the tradition of Newman, and far and away the best hopes for understanding the development of doctrine lie along the lines there indicated. But they seem a very modest conclusion from his daring statements about dogmas being a beginning and of their all being finite and therefore inadequate. The word "finite" is ambiguous, for by it we may mean something transient which looks elsewhere for its stability and truth, or we can in this context mean that we do not know as God knows; but to pass from the contrast to deny that man has a capacity for knowing truth, and absolute truth as well, is a fallacy. Moreover Rahner seems a little too attached to what is called the coherence view of truth. This view holds that the criterion of truth is its coherence. In strict logic such a view can never get off the ground, because if we start with a statement and then another different from it, neither can be true, since neither coheres. And this being so, a third statement has nothing to cohere with, and even supposing that it had, as cohering with only one of the first two statements, it would be partly incoherent. This may sound too like a game, but the theory deserves severe handling because we never do find a completely coherent reality, and therefore we are left uncertain whether as in a labyrinth we may not have taken the wrong turn near the end and may have to start all over again. Critics have assailed the arguments with examples: I can know the cards in my own hand without knowing what cards each of my opponents holds. I can know the address of the person to whom I am writing without knowing the necessary, immutable essence, but because the whole of salvation history is a progressive revelation of the way in which the free God who is active in history has wished to enter into relationship with his world." This is truly well said, even though a metaphysical idea of God is not tied down to that of a necessary immutable being. A metaphysic of persons and of love is probably a better way of approach to theology than the old Greek manner. In this one respect at least Greek thought showed very definite limitations.

The reconciliation of static and dynamic truth is brought nearer by these words of Rahner. He improves on his own idea when he adds that so far as Christian doctrine is concerned, "there is nothing more to come . . . but only the unveiling of what is already 'here' as his 'presence.'" Revelation is now closed, closed because paradoxically it remains open to the concealed presence of divine plenitude in Christ. So what he means by saying that a dogma is not an end but a beginning can be translated as follows: In Christ all is consummated; there is nothing more to be said after the Logos, the Word has been made flesh, and his Presence endures, waiting through time while mankind reads and rereads the words of life, and finds in them the Presence ever new. No wonder the Beloved Disciple ended his account by saying, "There are many other things which Jesus did, the which, if they should be written every one, I suppose that even the world itself could not contain the books which should be written. Amen."

Rahner's views, then, safeguard the absolute character of doctrines better than some of the contemporary writers whom I have quoted. Does he really do justice, however, to the identity which truths must keep despite the vagaries of time and place? Perhaps a distinction should be made between doctrinal and moral truths. The latter are bound up often with types of culture and circumstances. For instance, the much-talked of moral question of birth control. In days when so many children died at birth or were carried off by trite. A friend of mine once told me that on reading the words already known to him, "He loved me with an everlasting love," he was so overcome at the thought of being in God's mind from all eternity that he dwelt constantly on the words for three months. There are so many sayings of this kind which at one moment or another strike one with their full force. Sometimes one can read over and over again a sentence without much attention, a line of Shakespeare, for instance, and then hear it pronounced by another. Straightway it becomes a part of one's life, a possession forever. In this way unquestionably truths grow and take on at the same time an immortality. They are taken as mottoes or set at the head of chapters in a book or put into a book of great sayings. Each person has his favorites.

What is known to us in our everyday experience keeps growing, and we hand on from generation to generation what we have learned. In this way what has concerned man from his very origins, for example, his health, has come to be understood better and better, though it is the same subject always, and no doubt women in Mesopotamia and in the Andaman Islands, in rose-red cities half as old as time and in modern Los Angeles, spent much of the day talking about it. So too with what was once man's favorite animal, the horse. The Parthians knew much about horses, and so did the patrons and the betting fraternity in Constantinople in Byzantine days, though they knew less about their inner functions and the breeding of them than a modern vet. Religious doctrines, however, have to be treated separately. They have something to say about religious mysteries and about a God who, as the hymn says, is "Immortal, Invisible, God only wise, In light inaccessible hid from our eyes." Christian doctrines are still more specialized. They are centered around the Revelation of God in Jesus Christ,' and that Revelation has for object our salvation and the glorious end of union with God Himself. This very statement divulges the mystery which is attached to all religious truths. They have an aura and a dimension which escapes full description, and this it is which allows for a special kind of growth and involves time in the understanding of them. They are static and dynamic. They are static because they draw, so to speak, a circle around what is holy ground, a ground where God's Presence is and where His Word is. The circle, therefore, excludes and enables religious authority to declare what is outside the circle and therefore heresy. At the same time the circle, which may in time have new circles drawn within it to prevent the search for false relationships, leaves the depth of the wisdom of God to be pored over as in a deep well and enjoyed. Therefore on the objective side a doctrine has infinite riches to be explored, and on the subjective side we must look at man himself. Aristotle made a distinction which is of supreme importance in any discussion of how man grows in knowledge. Physical processes are all incomplete until the end of the process. When one sees the scientist in his laboratory there are various manifestations of shapes, sounds, rapid changes, but it is only at the end that he will point triumphantly to the product, which has taken so much time. On the level, however, of mind, in that higher plane or climate to which I have already referred, each step in the process has its value, and is in a sense complete. Aristotle pointed out that a rational being develops by means of his own acts of knowledge and choice, and each of these acts is complete in itself, what he calls *teleiai* in order to distinguish them from processes which reach perfection only at the end of the process. This holds for every human being once he or she has reached the age of reason. Before that their actions are only preparatory, as the work of a student is in preparation for an examination or the practices and rehearsals of a young ballet dancer before her first public appearance. In the examination and in the public appearance the performers bring all the student and artist have and are to the test. This is a full act, and will be judged as such. The grimmest example of this truth is that of a bullfighter, who takes his life in his hands each time he goes into the ring— as indeed a famous bullfighter declared at a dinner in his honor: "All we artists take our lives in our hands and commit ourselves utterly in each work of art." Now this special characteristic allows for fullness and development. In Christian teaching it is held that a man can commit an act of love such that if he dies he goes straight to heaven, even though he be of tender years and therefore apparently of an incomplete personality; and again he can commit so grave a sin as to deserve the loss of God's friendship. Here is an example where the self is static in that a man is properly himself when he acts freely or writes his ideas down, and yet he may go on growing for years and should grow in wisdom and moral perfection. He is a dynamism which is always capable of being static; he can talk truth at any moment, and can love like the young man in the Gospel, who was asked to give up all and follow Christ. The language here used is akin to that of the existentialists, and so they may be called in to testify—willing or unwilling—to this form of humanism.

Lastly there is the personal element to be considered in religious doctrine. It is used in a dialogue between God and the soul—a dialogue in which the subject, if not the vocabulary, has been proposed by God. Karl Rahner says with admirable insight that Christian theology does not arise from a curiosity to know what God is like, nor was Jesus Christ concerned to tell us more about God than what has helped for our salvation and love of God here upon earth. It is God, therefore, who reveals as much of Himself as is good for our well-being. It is a dialogue full of wisdom and love, and one in which we participate.

CHAPTER 5
CHRISTIANITY FRATERNIZING

The God whom atheists abandon is of mean conception and easily destroyed because He is in their own image.

The world awoke to find itself not Arian but barbarian.

Some theologians are difficult to see through; they follow Heidegger and have been greatly influenced by the first part of his name.

So far I have considered first the possibilities of a purely secular humanism, and then some attempts to show how Christianity, for example, should abandon its isolation and its supernatural character and work in with secular ideals. In discussing these possibilities certain contemporary assumptions had to be examined, the place of reason in religion and in a human society, whether some absolutes are required, or, instead, whether working hypotheses are sufficient, and finally an affiliated problem, that of the meaning and value of static and dynamic truth. In most modern views the importance of history has been emphasized, and even when Christianity has been given full acknowledgment, there is a tendency to tie it to history in a way which would have astonished not only a Father of the Desert or a Thomas à Kempis, but even a Bossuet or a Newman. In fact we see now in a theory such as that of Teilhard de Chardin a boxing of the compass from no association with the world to a close relationship.

Teilhard de Chardin is the outstanding example of this new arm-in-arm friendship. More akin to writers like P. de Cerveau are R. Marlé and Louis Dupré. They have the same desire to show the intimate connection between religious truths and history. A dogma, says R. Marlé ("*Le Dogme dans la Foi*," *Études*, January 1947) is usually an answer to a question, and the question is always of a specific kind in a historical surrounding. Hence history conditions our knowledge and partly determines the manner of its formulation. For this reason a dogma is always subject to reformulation, however difficult that may be in practice. Even Scripture is to some extent determined by its historical context; for though it is the Word of God it is also a historical document. Human nature is so constituted that men appropriate historically, that is, in the form of the culture in which they live, the sacred truth and saving grace which come from God. There is always the *"kairos,"* which cannot be forestalled nor treated as out of time. A bad habit has too long prevailed of ignoring the kairos or trying to fix it or exaggerate it. It is this bad habit which we see at work in the appeals to Scripture and the citing of texts out of their contexts to prove a religious argument. The immutability of dogma does not mean that it is static. Though the Church cannot err—for if it did, the guarantee of the protection of the Holy Spirit would be false—nevertheless truth can be fragmentary and partial, as seen by a St. Paul or a St. James. We do not possess the Word of God as we do some physical possession. We are rather like travelers on a journey, this time to eternity, and our baggage will suit the places we meet and stay at on the way. This is why we should look on dogma as news for the journey, a map for the region to be traversed. It is thus in its orientation and in its movement toward the goal that God's truth shows itself, as of old at Nicaea, Ephesus, and Trent.

In this journey there are some truths which are more central than others. The less central ones, as they deal with specific problems of the time, need a more considered analysis; for the Church may have given a thin picture of itself, by overelaboration, for example, by absenting itself from life in the world, or holding itself aloof from communism. All the time, nevertheless, the Church keeps its living identity, never confusing itself with the circumstances in which it has to express itself, nor with the prevailing ideas of the time. R. Marlé tells us, "The development of dogma is not the result of logical deduction starting from non-temporal truths. Nor is it uniquely an organic development, a progressive deepening grasp of its basic ideas. It is, rather, the expression of a life lived by the Church in time and directed to enlighten, guide and save men whose lives are radically bound up with history. Dogma and theology are not the same, though they are inseparate. The peripheral dogmas require more variety in theological explanations than the central ones." Theology relies on systematic explanation, which bears the mark of time, whereas dogma springs from the living confession of the faith. One can freely use any system, but if one puts it before the living faith, one falls into heresy.

Louis Dupré follows the same line of thought as R. Marlé, but in his own interesting and distinctive way. We have tended, he says, to treat history as a kind of moving receptacle for the static ideas of Revelation: and the reason for this is that the Christian religion is a dialogue of the creature with the Transcendent. It was initiated by a revelation from a transhistorical source. But this also happened to the Jews, and their religion had a history. Can any Revelation be definitive and final? Surely all statements are subject to development as man himself develops. The realistic answer, then, is that Revelation must be expressed adequately enough[1] to remain authoritative for later generations. Even Christ himself spoke within the limitations of a

[1] But who is to judge this? And if some truths can be expressed adequately, why not all?

particular time and place. "Christ is absolutely authoritative in what he expressed, and in that it was He, the God-Man, who expressed it. But his particular way of expressing it is, as all expressions are, co-determined by individual and cultural characteristics." What is true of Christ is still more true of the reports about him. The Gospels' authority springs from this, that their vision of Christ's teaching and acts is an inspired expression of the faith of the original Christian community.

As Christ himself and the Gospels are determined, so too the growth and declarations of dogmas. Again the authority of the words of Christ and the Church safeguard the definitions, but they also belong to history. They do at least have minimal adequacy in transmitting God's message effectively to later generations. Yet each generation has to capture the truth anew. But how can we be sure that we have God's truth? How can this historical determination and change co-exist with the absolute expressed once for all in Revelation? Dupré rejects the distinction of implicit and explicit truth as insufficient, and he also dismisses the view of Leslie Dewart that truth consists in constant conceptualizations. He falls back upon the power of the Church, through the work of the Holy Spirit, to keep in touch with the basic interpretations of the Christian tradition. It has in its power to look at facts and see them as religious facts and so accept, for instance, the Second Epistle of St. Peter as authoritative while rejecting the *Shepherd of Hermas* and the *Didache*.

Both these writers help us, I think, to see how Christianity can be called a truly historical religion, sharing in various cultures and playing its part in the development of civilization. They do this without compromising the claim of Christianity to belong to another world as well as to that of man making his own history in time. And indeed in safeguarding the dimension of the supernatural, the possibilities of man in the secular city are infinitely enlarged. One might object to many of the statements in their explanation of the development of doctrine. The main weakness in both accounts is, I think, in the failure to give adequate justification for the appeal to authority. In both authority comes in as a *deus ex machina,* because they hesitate to limit the degree of conditioning and determining of truth in the course of history.

No matter, because already in a preceding chapter the delicate subject has been examined, and in the meantime there awaits us the gigantic schema of Teilhard de Chardin to provide for a full humanism, both Christian and secular. His is by far the most comprehensive and grandiloquent effort to make peace between Christianity and the world, between the City of God and the City of Man. The general lines of his theory have become so familiar that there is no need to repeat them at any length. Besides, the theory has a simplicity which makes both the methods followed and the ideal presented easily intelligible. Until recently orthodox Christians fought shy of the hypothesis of evolution. It had from the Christian point of view an unfortunate start, as Thomas Huxley, perhaps its chief promoter after Darwin, was an agnostic. Bishop Wilberforce challenged Huxley and was worsted. But now Teilhard de Chardin wholeheartedly accepts evolution and makes it the mainspring of his theory. He had from childhood a passionate love of this earth, and later as we know he wrote of making it an altar whereon he could offer sacrifice to God. Nature is all one to him, and he, therefore, seemed never to have found any difficulty in the idea of the simplest form of matter evolving into animal and then human life. The process of evolving is from what is simple to what is complex—life is reached, and there we find individuals that are biologically close to one another; they form groups and periodically segmentate owing to chromosomic changes and the cumulative intensification of certain characteristics. Finally a new form of life develops, which has the unique characteristic of being able to look at itself and by its power of imaging to reflect upon itself and to reflect also what is outside. A new world is born, which contains all there is, in the tiny compass of human minds. This is *Homo sapiens*—and in the thousands of years of his existence, "in accordance with the most certain and the most universal of the laws of cosmic substance, man has grown in one way or another more complex, both organically and statistically, because it is exactly the same thing for a living group to propagate itself and to ramify." *Homo sapiens,* then, begins a new cycle, for all that has come into existence in the process of evolution can now be imaged out and conceived in the mind of this new species. Nature finds a spokesman for itself, who can tell its story. It finds also a priest who can give voice to its praise of its Creator. The human species as a unit is of a kind which tends to take the form of a centered unity; hence we see the gradual unification of mankind as cultures converge and produce a more universal one. But, as Teilhard de Chardin argues in the quotation just given, man does not stop at being a man, he is in process himself of passing into a higher species. In that species there will be a co-conscious society, more one than a swarm of bees, but keeping the perfection already achieved of personality. The process will be one in thought and love, held together by the truth they have discovered in the universe and the love they have for it and their Creator. In the language of Teilhard de Chardin, man is a species, which, because it is global and reflective, tends inevitably to knit itself together materially and psychologically so as to form biologically a new superorganism, one that will be both collective and personal. Man acquires the power of forming in the very heart of time and space a central and singular gathering point of the whole stuff of the universe. But' now for this new organism or species to be true to itself and the world and history, it in turn must be centered in and around One who is both the Alpha, the creative beginning, and the Omega, the final end and meaning of the cosmos. This is the cosmic Christ.

Such a system—or shall we say vision?—is bound to give rise to different interpretations according as it seems complete or only suggestive or just mythical. It can be weighed by scientists, philosophers, and theologians, and each is likely to have some reserves; thus, the scientist may brush aside the science of P. Teilhard but politely suggest he may be a philosopher. Scientists, in fact, are not agreed on Teilhard de Chardin's credentials or accuracy. There are those who reserve the name of scientist to scholars who in chemistry, physics, and biology, for example, work with intimate knowledge of the subject to establish new laws, and allow the name only out of politeness to the excavators and archeologists, in which group we place Teilhard de Chardin. They go on to say that "there are people who actually believe that Teilhard de Chardin had a claim to qualification as a biological scientist because he described some fossils and geological beds, on the strength of which, utterly ignorant of genetics, ecology, experiments in natural selection or molecular biology, he constructs a fairy tale of evolution, which some wishful thinkers have hailed as a synthesis of science and religion." Gilson and Maritain are equally severe, if more polite, as we shall see. De Chardin has been charged with being responsible for the view that Christianity and communism are natural allies. He is said to make little of the importance of individual persons in the interests of the "collectivity" he so much loves. God, too, as Creator must make room for a necessary world evolution from the lowest to the highest. Even the more moderate detect a tendency to subject Christ himself to this evolutionary movement, inasmuch as the cosmic Christ, who is the Omega to be, is on a higher level of development than the Son of Man, born in Bethlehem, who lived nearly two thousand years ago. There is too much Herbert Spencer and Julian Huxley, it is said, and too little of the orthodoxy of a John Chrysostom or an Augustine. His language is unusually abstract for a Frenchman; for example, he invents the name "noosphere" for a region of the mind where will be found a "harmonised collectivity of consciousness," equivalent to a sort of superconsciousness. The idea behind the word is that of "the earth not only becoming covered by myriads of grains of thought but becoming enclosed in a single thinking envelope so as to form functionally no more than a single vast grain of thought on the sidereal scale, the plurality of individual refractions grouping themselves together and reinforcing one another in the act of a single unanimous reflection" (*The Phenomenon of Man*). The difficulty of understanding this sentence is much increased by the use of images of thought and of an envelope of ideas and one grain on a sidereal scale, but also by the personalizing of the abstractions. It is bad enough for him to address evolution almost as if it were his brother or sister, and to praise its mighty works; when the personal abstractions begin to multiply, the result does begin to look like a myth for grown-ups.

Some theological critics can see little more in *The Phenomenon of Man* and the succeeding volumes than a spiritualized or sentimentalized form of materialism or pantheism. Progress is substituted for the God worshipped by Christians, and many of the Christian dogmas are watered down. There is an implicit denial of creation, original sin, and grace, it is said. Adam's choice in the Bible story appears to be regarded—in a letter to a friend, P. André Ravier—as "a statistically unavoidable by-product of a Universe in the process of unification with God." Sentences, too, which taken out of their context certainly sound strange, are also quoted against him, one such as the following in *Comment Je Crois*, which shows his deep love of all we mean by nature and human life: "If I lost my faith in Christ, in a personal God, in the Holy Ghost, I would still continue believing in the World. The first and last thing I believe in is the value, the infallibility and the goodness of the World. In the moment of my death, it is to this faith I shall abandon myself." This ought to please the humanists, and when joined with other views he expressed in letters, their effect is to turn Christian philosophers like Maritain and Gilson against him. Gilson declares his views to be theological fiction, and Maritain compares them to counterfeit money which drives out the good money. Maritain is influenced in his criticism by some of P. Teilhard's letters and by his mention of an *anima mundi,* a soul of the world. In one of these letters to Léonide Zanta we find him saying that "what dominates my interests" is to establish and "diffuse a new religion (call it a better Christianity, if you like) where the personal God ceases to be the great neolithic proprietor of recent times to become instead the soul of the world, which our religion and cultural stage of growth demand." This mention of a "soul of the world" leads Maritain to place Teilhard among the gnostics. I think, however, another interpretation is far more likely, and besides Maritain pays no attention to the words "our religion" later in the sentence. P. Teilhard, as already stated, had a semimystical intuition of the sacred quality of created nature, and this was reinforced by his sense of the presence of God. This was not gnosticism but a special gift of God. Even so his systematizing of this may have been a mistake, and Maritain is sure that it was. Teilhard de Chardin appropriated the scientific hypothesis of evolution and made it into a universal philosophy, a great myth of the cosmos with each item of the universe reaching beyond and above itself from the simplest to the highest, with Christ the beginning and the end—and all to the glory of God. In doing this, Maritain contends, he committed the great sin against the intellect of confusing together in total promiscuity different degrees of knowledge, the sensible, the mathematical, and the philosophical. We all know how important Maritain thought the distinction of these degrees to be, and therefore the result, in his judgment, was sure to be theological fiction about cosmic stuff and a cosmic Christ: the Christ of the Gospel is transformed into a Christ who is essentially *"évoluteur et humanisateur,"* "an unreal universal agent."

Gilson is equally adverse to this manner of philosophizing. Maritain quotes him in his *Paysan de Garonne*. Gilson tells how P. Teilhard spoke to him of the vital need today of analyzing and making precise the existential and relevant relations between Christ and the universe. "Our task is to make of Christ the Redeemer the Christ of Evolution and so integrate Christianity and Cosmogenesis." This means the assimilation of Christ to the cosmic force, the origin and end of evolution, and "the elevation of the historic Christ to a physical universal function." Such a view disturbed both Gilson and Maritain. They quote other passages which have a strange sound, about "panchristianising the Universe" and calling matter the stuff of spirit. They have found in Claude Tresmontant's *Le Père Teilhard de Chardin et la Théologie* and in Cardinal Journet's *Nova et Vetera* other passages to sharpen their opposition. I will content myself with only two, which bear on P. Teilhard's belief in a Christian humanism. "We realise that for created beings God is inevitably led to mingle with the multitude and incorporate himself therein"; and the second: "Fundamentally our Universe has always been (and no other kind of Universe can be thought of) one of good and evil hazards—that is to say, impregnated with evil, that is, in a state of original sin, that is, baptisable."

These quotations, while many would call them rash and inaccurate, do show his passionate belief in this world and human life in it. The extravagance, which Maritain and Gilson noticed, can be balanced by other passages which show his humble faith and orthodoxy despite the trials he had to endure. Let us not question his intentions. His life proved that he believed wholeheartedly the faith he practiced. What does remain uncertain is the compatibility of his grand schema with orthodox Christianity, and again to what degree he has succeeded in offering a workable Christian humanism and reconciling the City of God with the secular city. Now it may well be true that P. Teilhard did not deal adequately with religious doctrines such as original sin, sin in general, grace, and glory. He would have, if pressed, given as his apologia that he was writing as a scientist and drawing the lines of a theory of the universe and man in terms of the best scientific thought.[2] By no means would all scientists agree with him on this; but granted his position it is for his followers, who see a fresh and far-seeing set of ideas contained in Teilhard de Chardin's writings, to work over the incomplete or inadequate or even erroneous sections and point out whether they can be amended so as to fit in with what is the essential in Teilhard de Chardin's vision. Some of the criticisms we can already see to be light and to rest on a misunderstanding. Both Maritain and Gilson make a strong point of the difference between the cosmic Christ, who is the Alpha and Omega, giving coherence and stability to the new species, the superorganism, and the Christ of Nazareth and Calvary, who lived two thousand years ago and was so poignantly human. At first the criticism seems very just and to break Teilhard de Chardin's theory in two. If man is developing into a higher species, how can the very life and center of this new higher species be identical with One who belongs to a lower species and comes only in what may be about the midpoint in the history and development of the lower species? Not only must the two figures be separate, but the super-Christ is not what we desire. The Christ of the Gospels answers all our needs and he wished to do so. "Come to me all ye that labor and are burdened and I will refresh you." But if we pause for a moment to realize who Christ is—not only man but God—

[2] *Vide* Teilhard de Chardin, *The Vision of the Past* (New York: Harper & Row, 1967).

then already he is far superior to any super-Christ of a higher species. He is already the Alpha, and in his Second Coming will show himself the Omega, "in whom all things are constituted."

These words of St. Paul do justify, I think, the language of Teilhard de Chardin. Indeed St. Paul's vision is one which Teilhard de Chardin might well have borne constantly in mind. It is quite orthodox and Pauline to make the Incarnation the resilient center of all history and even the universe. The Word in the Bible means the dynamic aspect of the God whose life is inaccessible to our hooded eyes, and the Word makes all to come together as in a book or work of art. It is this aspect of the Lord which St. Paul had in mind when he called him the First Born and the Lord in whom all things are constituted. "In Him all created things took their being, heavenly and earthly, visible and invisible. . . . They were all created through Him and in Him: he takes precedency of all and in Him all subsist" (Letter to the Colossians).

P. Teilhard does not say anything so gloriously extravagant as St. Paul. If we adopt a less exacting view of evolution, a remote but real similarity comes to light between the superorganism of Teilhard de Chardin's and the perennial doctrine in the Church of sanctifying grace. Through the splendor of this grace man is reanimated on a higher level of being and his body is to be restored and reintegrated into that of the risen Christ. This to some will seem, while vague, nevertheless more acceptable a vision of the future of man than Teilhard de Chardin's. He has tied it to a theory of evolution, and moreover has without warrant, I believe, postulated a further evolution of man from his present species to a higher one. To judge from the verdicts of distinguished scientists, such as René Dubos, there is no evidence whatever for this hypothesis. What is observable in history and from anthropological and archeological searches is the development from primitive man through stages of savagery to cultures, and within measurable time the gradual coming together of the peoples of the world perforce by economics, language communication, and the reduction of distance as a separating factor. What P. Teilhard hopes for, namely, a union of mankind by means of a common knowledge and truth and goodwill, will only intensify strictly human relations and so prepare the way for the coming of the Christ St. Paul describes. P. Teilhard does not here make use of St. Paul, and therefore, somewhat strangely, he finds that the historical Christ creates a problem for him. He cannot understand a Christ who would be smaller than the world, the vast consistency of the world, and so he looks to a "new cosmological, anthropological and theologico-Christological Hexameron to fit the dimensions of our new consciousness of the world."

Granted that some of the difficulties raised against Teilhard de Chardin can be answered or smoothed over or corrected, there do remain others which stand in the way of a confident acceptance of his views. They are so serious that it will be well to separate off various problems to which he is supposed to have given answers. One would be: has P. Teilhard offered a genuine reconciliation between science and religion? Another would be: does he provide an open sesame for a Christian humanism? Thirdly, a question intimately connected with that of humanism, but differently orientated: does he succeed in changing the picture of the true or typical Christian saint?

To begin with praise, despite all the opposition P. Teilhard encountered and the criticisms he has evoked, the general sentiment seems to be that he performed a great task, and that like Moses striking the rock he has provided water for a thirsty generation, a generation thwarted by the narrow philosophies of the day, the economic and political tightening grip on human initiative and activities, and the hard technical specialization of the sciences. P. Teilhard, to change the image, has stood up, blessed the earth we stand on, envisoned a supreme ideal for man, and opened vistas wherethrough we can see the promised land. This makes of him an outstanding figure: but it is quite another matter whether any one of the lines of his solution leads anywhere. I was once told by a great scholar that Henry Nettleship's book on Epigraphy was a classic of the first order: he added that hardly a single word in it was correct.[3] Certain writers have their hallmarks and it is difficult to efface them, but then I remember that even a Paracelsus can do that. Sir Peter Medawar rates P. Teilhard lower than Paracelsus, but his complete lack of sympathy weakens his criticism. P. Teilhard apparently never asked himself what evolution could mean outside the conventional sense as used in a particular science. There an observable relationship is set up and the closeness of it is subject to calculation. But, if one asks what precisely it is which "comes to be," remaining itself as it begins to change, the scientist shrugs his shoulders to signify that that is a philosophical question outside his province. It is convenient to get around difficulties which occur within the subject matter itself of the science by employing words like "emergent" or "jumps." P. Teilhard, however, follows the example of Sir Julian Huxley, who invented the word "mentoid" in order to combine mind and matter even in the simplest elements of nonliving matter. This is saved from being mumbo-jumbo because of a methodological supposition of a unity running through the world we know from the lowest to the highest. P. Teilhard adopts the same idea of there being latent mind in every particle of matter. This is as eerie as the view of some simple pantheists that everything is divine and therefore, in some sense of the word, I must be sitting on God when I sit in a chair. It is quite impossible to live such theories. Only a madman would treat a piece of carbon as a silkworm or honeybee deserves to be treated; and as for

[3] I have heard a similar criticism of Wittgenstein.

those who refuse to take life, how can they manage to survive in a world where I suppose everything is living and forbidden? It is hard to see how such a theory can make any sense, for it belongs to the genre of storytelling, where centaurs and mermaids are to be seen, and djinns spring out of bottles. Almost equally hard is it to understand how the lower gives rise to the higher, though Tyndall in the early bloom of evolution could rhapsodize on the wonder of Newton and Shakespeare preexisting in some early gaseous liquid. St. Thomas Aquinas, to take a leading Christian representative theologian, remained unperturbed by the suggestion that life might proceed from the nonliving. All orthodox theologians, however, contested the hypothesis that the human soul could fit in with the evolutionary theory, unless "jumps" were admitted. Nowadays, it must be said, there is not the same unanimity on the subject, but P. Teilhard fails to explain how it could happen.[4]

[4] The supporters of P. Teilhard have rallied to his defense, but I do not see how out of the material he has given us they can make a bona fide case. At the critical points he likes to use an idea of his own which the scientific record does not warrant, or, what is worse, would rule out as nonscientific. He is confident, for example, that there is a convergence in nature toward unity. He justifies this partly by what he calls "extrapolation," that is, by reading back into earlier stages what is present in a higher stage. Man is self-conscious, reflective. But what is a character at the top must also be a character lower down. Therefore, the syllogism goes, there is some kind of consciousness in the most elementary units of matter. This argument seems to rely on the conclusion in order to reach it. The same kind of argument is used with the distinction of inner and outer, which is applied to energy. Human beings have an inner and outer life and therefore all that precedes hominization must also have an interior and an exterior. This makes the word "inner" carry far too great a weight. An inner life has a limit within living things. Outside them it is a metaphor or a matter of spatial distinction. There is an inside and an outside to a piece of copper; break it and what is outside and inside have changed their relation, and that is all. Yet on the strength of this distinction P. Teilhard works out a law of the more complexity the more consciousness: he invents a theory of orthogenesis, and hap-

Such matters at any rate can be ignored here because the dispute is irrelevant to the question of a Christian humanism. In P. Teilhard's account of man's ascension there is a strong note of optimism. For one who sees evolution moving on and upward from man to a still higher species this is natural. On the other hand, this optimism as resting on a natural, and therefore one would surmise, an almost inevitable process, seems fanciful and not in accordance with the evidence. As already stated, biologists do not contemplate a new species or superorganism, and P. Teilhard himself would find it extremely difficult to make precise what he means by a superhuman organism. For this reason among others I think the answer to the first question is already forthcoming: in a theory bound up so closely with a philosophy of evolution, I do not think we have the wherewithal for a reconciliation between science and religion. Furthermore, the strict scientist may be alienated by P. Teilhard's broad generalizations about nature and man and superorganisms: and if a scientist is scandalized, how much more the philosopher, who is a detective of the fallacies in language; and finally, one has to shuffle his religious cards to make any kind of partnership practical. The optimism, for instance, in the Christian religion is based not on man but on the saving power of Christ and God's grace as given to man. Even so, that complete success will attend man's

---

pily points the direction ever upward as though to the scientist nature had ever anything to say to that. Not only this, but he invents another distinction between radial and tangential energy. The first is responsible for increase and multiplication within a phylum, and the second for those unaccountable leaps. Moreover, by this distinction he thought he could escape the supposed running down of the material world—for that which is the conscious tangential inner energy counteracts entropy as it is not subject to it. I believe that P. Teilhard is partly mistaken here. What he is saying, however, is so far removed from the mechanistic, naturalistic Lamarckian or Darwinian understanding of evolution that criticism on the old grounds may be irrelevant or unfair.

efforts is not assured. It depends on man's free will and his acceptance of the loving invitation of Christ to a life of supreme happiness. P. Teilhard does recognize this, and owns that by misuse of his freedom man might bring about catastrophe, but these are asides and seem to me soon forgotten in the swell of enthusiasm for a new earth and a new heaven. Many who have grown despondent may respond to P. Teilhard's magnetic enthusiasm, and so pay little attention to the multiple apparent evidence of growing irreligion in the world and the widening antagonism of communism and Western civilization. Karl Rahner suggests that Christians are coming to be a "diaspora" in an irreligious world. In view of the 700 million atheists in China and the 300 million in the Soviet empire, and the outlook in India and Africa, it is difficult to be as optimistic as de Chardin. There are grim texts in the Gospels as well as optimistic ones, for when Christ comes again, "Where will he find faith upon earth?" The signs of the end as given in the Gospels belong to apocalyptic and eschatological literature, and therefore are not to be taken too literally as referring to real events. Nevertheless their tenor is one of a battle between Christ and Antichrist, with false prophets abounding and evil apparently triumphant. Such texts must be counted as against a supposedly scientific vision of things to come, when science and religion will be in perfect harmony.

What then of the second question, the possibility of Christian humanism? Undoubtedly P. Teilhard has created a new hope and opened a new world full of possibilities. The actual form it has taken, the program which he presents, may not be one which either the Christian or the humanist will accept as it stands. I do not think that it brings religion down into the marketplace or will have anything very much to say to individuals in their own private lives. In this respect it compares poorly with Harvey Cox's *The Secular City:* it does not get down to brass tacks, or advertise itself like one of Cecil B. De Mille's movies. This may be a blessing, and if we look for quality, then Cox's program seems hardly better than a piece of salesmanship for Macy's or a Ford motorcar, whereas P. Teilhard resembles one of the prophets intent on leading his beloved people on the way of righteousness into a country flowing with milk and honey. Through all his writings the personality of P. Teilhard shines out, and it is this which first convinces the reader that an exceptional highway to perfection is being offered to him, one which embraces not only himself but every human being, and not only every human being but the whole of nature, the universe itself. No one who has read the *Divine Milieu* can help admiring both the genius and the spirituality of the writer, and at the same time his intense humanity. He is made aware of a rare kind of human being who has a mystic love of nature and feels the presence of God everywhere. He loved God and he loved nature, a more rare combination than is usually realized, and miraculously he included human beings also, for themselves and not just as means, rungs in a ladder leading to God. As he wrote: "To divinize is not to destroy but to create anew. We will never know all that the Incarnation still looks for from the powers of the world. We can never hope enough from the growth of human unity. Lift up your head, Jerusalem! See the immense crowd of those who build and those who search. In the laboratories, in the studios, in the deserts, in the workshops, in the vast social crucible do you see them, these men who toil? Well then all that is astir through them in art, science and thought, all that is for you. Come open your arms and your heart, and like Jesus, your Lord, gather in the torrent, the deluge of the power that flows in men."[5] In the *Divine Milieu* he tries to say something about the divine Presence in the world. He gives five headings, or circles as he calls them,

[5] I take this from an article on Teilhard de Chardin by Pierre Reginald Crea, O.P.

which bear a remarkable resemblance to the Contemplation on Divine Love which St. Ignatius of Loyola plans at the end of his famous manual, *The Spiritual Exercises.* In the first circle we realize the divine immanence; we taste the Omnipresence in all things. In the second, we see the unifying action of that Presence. God in whom all things subsist is their consistency. In the third, we see how "it is God's action," his energy, "that shapes us like the clay of the first day." The fourth is where we realize that the history of the cosmos is a history of divinization, and that our task is to help in the fashioning of it. Lastly, in the fifth circle, "I have seen a shadow passing by. . . . What is the name of this mysterious Entity, which is a little our work and with which above all we commune; which is something of ourselves and which, nevertheless, holds us in subjection; which has need of us to be, and which at the same time dominates us with his whole Absolute? . . . I feel it. It has a name and a face. But it alone can reveal itself and give its name as . . . Jesus."

P. Teilhard's friend, P. de Lubac, quotes him as saying "that I would like to be able to have a great love of Christ in the very act of loving the Universe. . . . Besides union with God and union with the world, is there not a union with God through the world?" It is the language, and the feeling that it expresses his very soul, which makes Teilhard de Chardin so attractive to the modern generation. He represents and makes vocal an inarticulate desire of so many to discover meaning in the universe, a direction to human life, and the humanizing of science. On reading him so many again have felt that he has opened a new vista. He is not at all writing a "dotty, euphoristic kind of nonsense" as Sir Peter Medawar, far from the madding crowd, stonily thinks. But granted the inspiration, are the system of ideas he has invented and the methods he has employed valid? As we have seen, Maritain and Gilson and many others think not. From the criticisms I have already given,

I suggest that though what P. Teilhard has written is not just fiction or false money, it should all the same be treated as a preface, an inspirational program rather than the beginning of a successful reconciliation of science, humanism, and religion. *C'est magnifique, mais ce n'est pas la guerre.*

What then of the third question, concerning Christian spirituality? It is here there is good reason to think that P. Teilhard will hold an important place in the history of Christian spirituality and as a chief sponsor of Christian humanism. He has put in a way which cannot be forgotten a view which some of us, in a more humble and less successful fashion, have tried to express. He brings the world and human life fully into the Christian rule of life. He removes that suspicion of the world which has governed spiritual teaching for centuries and widened the rift between the City of God and the City of Man. He is not the only one to try to do this, and without fully understanding the justification for so acting the present generation has decided that the best way, if not the only way, to find God is to love one's neighbor and be active in good works. P. Teilhard writes in large letters the charter for this. As so often, he may have leaned too much to the other side, and that will be discussed in the next chapter. What is unquestionable is that he stands at the parting of the ways, saying that one way which used to be forbidden because it led away from God—to be shunned therefore as in Bunyan's *Pilgrim's Progress*—is a disused highway to the City of God.

He tells us how he came to this view. "The originality of my belief is that it has its roots in two spheres of life which are usually looked upon as being mutually antagonistic. By education and intellectual formation I belong to the children of heaven. But by temperament and professional studies I am 'a child of the earth' . . . I have set up no dividing wall. . . . After thirty years devoted to the pursuit of inner unity, I have the impression that a synthesis has taken place, in a natural way, between the two streams that make their demands upon me." In *Christologie et Évolution* he puts the problem succinctly, and his answer:

To adore formerly meant preferring God to things, by referring them back to him and sacrificing them for him. To adore now has come to mean pledging oneself body and soul to the creative act, by associating oneself with it, so as to bring the world to its fulfilment by effort and research. . . . Loving one's neighbour formerly meant not defrauding him and binding up his wounds. Charity, from now on, while not ceasing to be imbued with compassion, will find its fulfilment in a life given for the common advance. Being pure formerly meant, in the main, standing aside and preserving oneself from stain. Tomorrow chastity will call above all for a sublimation of the powers of the flesh and of all passion. Being detached formerly meant not concerning oneself with things and only taking from them the least possible. Being detached now means step-by-step moving beyond all truth and beauty by the power of the very love that one bears for them. Being resigned formerly could signify a passive acceptance of the present conditions of the Universe. Being resigned now will be no longer allowed save to the warrior fainting away in the arm of the angel.

Not all the contrasts he makes here seem to be fair, but the general indictment of the past has enough truth in it to warrant our calling his own view revolutionary—a decisive moment in the history of Christian spirituality. He himself called it a synthesis, and many of us who have been brought up on the classical spiritual books and read the message of the spiritual writers of the nineteenth century have felt the onesidedness of the teaching and tried to find a solution. But it is P. Teilhard who has put it into cosmic terms, and there is no gainsaying their importance. What now remains is to examine their validity and come to a conclusion about the form, if any, which a Christian humanism should take.

CHAPTER 6

THE CHRISTIAN
VIEW
OF LIFE

"When the wine of natural joy
is spent and there is nothing left but the water of affection, then doth
Christ turn the water into wine."

(FRANCIS ROW, *Mystical Marriage*)

"The tree upon which was fixed the limbs of Him dying was ever the
chair of the Master teaching." (ST. AUGUSTINE OF HIPPO)

"It is more easy to come to the knowing of God than to know our own
soul. For our soul is so deep grounded in God . . . that we may
not come to know thereof, till we have first knowing of God."

(DAME JULIANA OF NORWICH)

Both Teilhard de Chardin and Harvey Cox are radically
optimistic when they look at the future; but so differently
do they regard it that the success of Cox's secular city
would mean the end and destruction of all P. Teilhard
stands for. The busy hum of Wall Street typewriters and
electronic gadgets and gas stations on whirling highways
would seem to him like the traffickers in the temple.
There is no new species in sight there—rather the likeli-
hood of subhuman life and activity, if we are to look at the
evidence and the statistics of the Kinsey Report and also
the reports on the spread of crime where it is possible to
collect the evidence. This evidence, unfortunately, hits
both Cox and P. Teilhard as well—and it is felt to be the

more regrettable, the higher and nobler the vision and the more human a happiness promised. We have grown callous, having had to listen to on the radio or read in the newspapers of the horrible brutalities happening not on a battlefield or in supposedly still savage countries, but next door and in times of relative prosperity. It needed the skill of Truman Capote's *In Cold Blood* and of Pamela Hansford Johnson's *Iniquity* to bring home to us the spreading indifference to human life and the murderous instincts still prevailing.

Both Cox and Teilhard de Chardin would no doubt point to the long and relatively constant growth of humanity, that growth which is used by the modern humanist as proof of man's high degree of self-sufficiency. This growth also convinced Bonhoeffer that religion can now well take a back seat as its ministrations are no longer needed. If, however, we look at this growth, it does not provide comforting evidence. Materially we are much better off than primitive peoples, and even than the civilizations of the near past, though we are often shocked out of our complacency to learn of the clean habits of the Romans and immemorially of the Japanese, and the presence of heating systems and drains at Knossos and other places. These are trifles, and other optimists with greater relevance point to the growth of democracy and the gradual leveling down of privilege and high quality to suit the needs of everyone in a state. Music has grown richer, painting and sculpture have rid themselves of unessentials and look only to their own aesthetic ends; economics is closer to being a science, and science itself has made prodigious steps. True, but leaving aside comparisons in art, how far has this meant that man is more moral, more fraternal, and truly free and happy? The more that is given the more does he expect, and the more that is given the less gratitude is felt. Only a cynical Diogenes in his tub would deny the blessings that have come through the removal of slum conditions, through living wages and health centers. The condition of the poor in the past was a disgrace to our humanity, even though it had its compensations in neighborliness and the consolations of shared hardship. There is a kind of law which makes what is almost intolerable a source of comradeship, the comradeship of the trenches and the desert, of Captain Scott and his four companions, or the *Kon Tiki* adventure. This of course is no excuse for the oppression of the poor in the past nor for the horrors of life in the Russian Butyri, the "conveyor-belt" whose object was "to wear out nerves, weaken the body, break resistance, and force the prisoner to sign whatever is required."[1] "Good to sleep, Better to be a stone."

Such inhuman conditions are mentioned because they are contemporary and serve as evidence of the plight of victims, and for who knows how long? But it is the modern failure of well-intentioned efforts which reveal best how man will not be satisfied. A government, as I write, is demanding equality in education and living conditons and wealth for all, and it proudly points to its achievements; but just at that very moment dockers are showing bitter resentment and coming out in an unofficial strike and so damaging themselves and their country. It is this flagrant contrast between material prosperity and contentment of soul that makes the planning for a well-run city as man's panacea by Harvey Cox so absurd. It is often said that the rich are most unhappy. Such a statement has never been verified, and is probably not more than a half-truth, if that; but Aldous Huxley did put his finger on a weak spot in any rich society. There is no risk, no adventure, no resistance to overcome. He said life would be so dull for the children of the rich. "The speed, the struggle, the one man fury are not for them." The very pleasures, too, which people take or indulge in tend to benumb and splinter the self, and

[1] Eugenia Ginzburg, *Into the Whirlwind* (New York: Harcourt, Brace & World, 1967), p. 69.

their level goes down, what with broken marriages, night-clubs, striptease, wrestling shows, pornography. We are, so it is said, living in a post-Christian culture, one far from the ideal contemplated by Teilhard de Chardin, and less and less is heard in schools and universities of the ideals of morality and religious life. Where, as in the case of the Peace Corps or Moral Rearmament or Oxfam, these ideals are put in the forefront, one feels that that is a reaction of the few caused by the general moral paralysis and the scorn for the saving virtues of patriotism, altruism, and self-sacrifice.

This has to be said, if we are to pass judgment on the new order of life which P. Teilhard believes is being ushered in. We all would like to clap our hands and salute a newcomer dressed as P. Teilhard wants him to be. Another contemporary prophet, Marshall McLuhan, who also like P. Teilhard has his severe critics, seems to blow hot and cold on ideals such as "traditional Christianity" has promoted. This, I think, is not for want of admiration for them: but what, he thinks, is going to determine the future is the changeover from a visual literary culture to an age fathered by electric media. McLuhan, to bring out his belief in a change in our human environment, quotes the controversial book, *Preface to Plato* by Eric Havelock. Part of this book's argument is that Greeks before the time of Plato were not a literary people, that is to say, the written word did not play a predominant part in their culture. Their culture relied on memory, on the spoken word. It was after the manner of a tribal life; they had grown up by means of a tribal encyclopedia. Hence the pre-Socratic thinkers have been interpreted wrongly. But with "the advent of individual detribalized man, new education was needed. Plato devised such a programme for literate man. . . . Education by classified data has been the Western programme ever since." After the discovery of printing this form of education, that of the eye and the written word, triumphed completely. But now it has been challenged, and because once again sound, voices, radio, television, and all the other electronic devices have ousted reading, it is no longer the same human environment. We are now back to a tribal, co-conscious society far more sophisticated than the primitive one, but equally immersed and equally dedicated.

This marks the change to a new "phase of the extension of man"—perhaps the final one, despite Harvey Cox and Teilhard de Chardin—"the technological simulation of consciousness, when the creative process of knowing will be collectively and corporately extended to the whole of human society, much as we have already extended our senses and our nerves by the various media." This sounds not unlike the superorganism of P. Teilhard, but McLuhan goes on to say that "whether the extension of consciousness, so long sought by advertisers for specific products, will be a good thing is a question that admits of a wide solution." No wonder, because the extension spoken of is a flat one: he mentions none of the heights of knowledge and love and nothing of the coherence of it all in the Word, who is both Alpha and Omega. Moreover, as the "message is the massage" the contents cease to be as important as the form, and this is imposed on modern society without its consent or without its full realization. There is, however, to be one community. "As electrically contracted the globe is no more than a village. Electric speed in bringing all social and political functions together in a sudden implosion has heightened human awareness of responsibility to an intense degree."

Few critics go all the way with Marshall McLuhan, and he himself gathers his ideas into such a serendipity shop that his writing has only a suggestive value. What, for instance, in fact would the changeover from a literary environment to one in which we are played upon by all the senses really entail? He relies upon a writer like Professor Eric Havelock for evidence of the state of mind of preliterary Greece, where the evidence is scanty and open to more than one interpretation. After Plato we have all the centuries when the majority of people, even the aristocrats, could not write or read. Literacy was a privilege of the clerks. Nevertheless there is no such marked difference in their habits from those of the eighteenth and nineteenth centuries. Chaucer and Dante are still close to us. McLuhan pays insufficient attention to that remarkable power all living things have—possibly owing to the struggle for existence—of adapting themselves without radical change to new conditions, as in a small way the human body so quickly adapts itself when we lose or gain five hours flying to and from the United States and Europe. All education can be called learning to adapt our minds to ideas and facts which are strange to us. It is true that there are media which affect us day and night without our being aware of their effect at the time; but as the body can give innumerable kinds of signals to warn us of change, so in daily experience we check what we are doing and thinking whenever a decision has to be made. We are not such victims of fate; we do not drown without a struggle when we are plunged into a new medium, like water. As Christopher Ricks has written, "A newspaper is not only a montage which replaces continuity by simultaneity and so presents the globe in juxtaposition 'cramped into a planisphere'—it has news." And the news is what ultimately counts, as the good news of eternal life of the Gospel has directed people in every century A.D. and in every climate and country, literate or illiterate, along lines which never deviate. Lastly, I wonder what McLuhan would have to say about Tony Last reading Dickens to Mr. James Todd of Brazil in *A Handful of Dust?*

Marshall McLuhan claims that the effect of this auditory revolution is to set up a new relationship, a new tribal society—"tribal," however, in a secular city way. "The circuited city of the future . . . will take on a totally new meaning under conditions of very rapid movement. It will be an information megalopolis." And again, this time under the inspiration of James Joyce: "The Finn cycle of tribal institutions can return in the electric age, but if again, then let's make it a wake or awake or both. Joyce could see no advantage in our remaining locked up in each cultural cycle as in a trance or dream. He discovered the means of living simultaneously in all cultural modes while quite conscious." The modern prophets foresee this new tribal society, McLuhan, Gerald Heard, and others, as well as Teilhard de Chardin.

The evidence for this does support the theory of a converging society to some extent, for, as already pointed out, almost every place in the world is near our doorstep; communication by language as well as by travel is far easier, and science with its technological applications and banks and giant corporations makes for an interdependence of nations. Does such a process of unification indicate a new humanism, and can Christianity play any significant part in it? The secular humanists would applaud the new federation of man, without admitting Christianity into it: Harvey Cox would see Christianity as best expressed in a well-run secular city, and Teilhard de Chardin sees what is best in man coming steadily to the fore and attaining a unique unity in Christ.

The weaknesses in P. Teilhard's vision have already been noticed, but bècause it so far surpasses the other hopes and prophecies of the future it will always inspire the humanist to believe in new possibilities of peace and happiness for man and to work for them. Depression, however, is in the air. All that the Christian Pavilion at the admirable Expo '67 in Montreal could do was to separate off three zones: one, the mirror of life today, the second, the evil that man has committed, and third, a Christian message of hope. Visitors there have spoken of the rather doleful impression conveyed, a hope that was bleak, and all the comfort contained in a few Biblical texts so little prominent that many failed to notice them. P. Teilhard's *Phenomenon of Man* and the books which succeeded it were strong in life, but so optimistic that by reaction one looked at the record of man and the promises now visible in the contemporary scene and saw little to justify any soaring hope for the future. Instead one was made conscious of a grave defect in his views. He looks to the future and all his hope is there. Marx also put all his eggs in one basket which had not yet been made. Both he and Teilhard de Chardin had a messianic expectation, and in this they fell far short of the reality, and were remiss in disregarding the countless persons who have lived and are now dead. Christianity takes in all time and all men, and its good news was as true a thousand years ago as now, and in a sense it had completed its mission. Teilhard de Chardin did not heed the eschatological element in the Christian message. Every generation is the end of the world. With the coming of Christ the world reached its fulfillment, and all that remains is to reap the rich harvest and to explore the many-splendored beauty of the Christ life, reflected and realized in new human aspects in one generation after another and continually unique. Nothing ultimate has been lost because one has lived in A.D. 500 or A.D. 1500 or A.D. 2000. Like circles in a tree's trunk, the tree grows but the same life is there within each circle.

That does not, however, prevent the future showing a closer and better intercourse between the religious Christian way of life and that of the secular world. It is here, I think, that the work of David Jones fits in and enables us to see how it is possible for the two to give light to each other. David Jones is the poet and painter of the sacramental value of all created things. This sacramental value is made very definite by the way all the signs are gathered up around the Eucharistic mystery, the Christian act which is both sign and bodily real. As Stuart Piggott[2] the prehistorian

[2] In *Agenda* (William Cookson, ed. London, Spring–Summer, 1967), p. 78.

says: "David Jones does not let poetic treasure trove go un-
claimed: like the Crown in law, he steps in as *ultima haeres*
to the deposits and brings them splendidly to light. He ex-
plores poetic deposits with the anxious care of the good ex-
cavator (far better than Schliemann 'who dug nine sites
down in Helen's laughless rock') alert for the unexpected
feature, the illuminating oddness, the links that bind culture to culture." Another writer, N. K. Sandars,[3] writes
that "eye, ear and understanding are equally engaged by a
brilliant mosaic of languages: the groups of words like
enamel cloisons, or the tiny miniatures on the cover of a
reliquary, are in their parts intense infusions of our several
inheritances, blended to the one inheritance." "The ar-
chaic smile of the Kouros is on the face of the 'numbed and
scurvied top-tree boy' on the ship bound for Albion from
Corbulo, and a sea shanty swings us past Langland's Rose
the dish-seller and the Cockney Lady of the Pool to the
ultimate mysteries of the Mass."[4] Or again—as it is only
by examples that we can see how all earthly things and
human actions pass into signs—"David Jones poet and
painter, sees things and paints them. Doric and Ionic and
Corinthian columns, all the ages of Greece and Rome, are a
background to the parenthetic travail of Aphrodite. The
past is all a now, the eternal in the petal, tree branches in
the clay of the teapot and in the brittleness of glass. The
earth herself in her alert pain dreams of the hand that has
shaped her. Nor man nor place stands alone. The scapegoat
of Israel is caught in the barbed wire of 1915 . . ."[5]

We live in the present day in conditions when "lost liter-
atures from Sumer to Mexico now jostle with Greece and
Rome; we can hear, if we wish, the songs of the eskimos
and the pygmies, while the traditions of the visual arts no
longer begin where we used to think they did, but come
from mud walls in Anatolia, rock walls in France, and from

[3] Sandars, *Agenda*, p. 96.
[4] Piggott, *Agenda*, p. 77.
[5] M. Saunders Lewis, *Agenda*, p. 91.

heaps of extinct animal bones in Austria or Moravia. The rocks themselves and the beginnings of life have lengthened still more the view."[6] This is after P. Teilhard's heart, and suggests the wonders of the earth waiting to be baptized. But while this knowledge now is with us at the level of the card index, it has in a way destroyed the simple familiarity to be found in one small culture or tradition. We now are finding a lodging but not a home in the great city, the technopolis of Harvey Cox. As Sandars remarks, "Everything is flying apart like our universe itself according to one interpretation because 'the centre cannot hold.' In general, the well-made objects, the right actions are presented to us as scattered, too soon dissipated, too small, tiny gestures quickly lost." But David Jones finds the clue to an answer, and that answer lies in his sacramental view of the universe. In "Art and Sacrament"[7] he writes that no sooner does a person "put a rose in his buttonhole but what he is already in the tripwire of sign, and he is deep in an entanglement of signs if he sends that rose to his sweetheart Flo: or puts it in a vase by her portrait: and he is hopelessly and up to the neck in that entanglement of Ars sign, sacrament should he sit down and write a poem 'about' that sweetheart. Heaven knows what his poem will really be 'about', for then the 'sacramental' will pile up by a positively geometric progression." Here then is an example of sign and sacrament, and we can see how to David Jones religion and daily life, the past and the present, are combined. To him they all fall around the Eucharist. To vary the image, one can think of a tree, a tree of life, on whose branches all kinds of birds perch and make love to each other, horses and cattle rest in its shade, and lovers scratch their names upon its bark. "This means," as Aneirin Talfan Davies writes,[8] "the thorough acceptance of the

[6] Sandars, *Agenda*, p. 95.
[7] In *Catholic Approaches* (New York: Farrar, Straus and Cudahy, 1955), pp. 210 ff.
[8] Davies, *Agenda*, p. 172.

physical universe, redeemed by God, through the Incarnation of His Son 'born of the Virgin Mary.' This, in turn, means the acceptance of the sacramental principle, which means the transformation of matter into means of grace for people—the creatures of God." Such a view is far from that of the secular city regarded simply as the only basis for operations by man and as capable of satisfying all his desires. To the commuter to the city, to the big shot in his office surrounded by telephones, to the citizen sitting at night and watching television, in the atomic, socialized, bureaucratic megalopolis of the future, signs and sacraments might seem irrelevant. But the revolt of the existentialists, the escape of the hippies *et hoc genus omne,* are met by a deeper understanding of the universe and a prayer which goes up in different forms in every age. David Jones says it in his own way:[9]

> Queen of the differentiated sites, administratrix
> of the demarcations, let our cry come unto you
>   In all times of imperium save us when the
> *mercatores* come save us
>   from the guile of the *negotiatores* save us
> from the *missi,* from the agents
>   who think no shame
> by inquest to audit what is shameful to tell
>   deliver us . . .

When they

>   number the souls of men
>   notch their tallies false
> disorder what they have collated,
> When they proscribe the diverse uses and impose the
> rootless conformities, pray for us
>   When they sit in Consilium
> to liquidate the holy diversities
>   Mother of particular perfections
>   Queen of otherness
>   Mistress of asymmetry

[9] Jones, *Agenda,* pp. 20 ff.

patroness of things counter, parti, pied, several
protectress of things known and handled
help of things familiar and small
　　　　　　wardress of the secret crevices
　　　　　　of things wrapped and hidden
mediatrix of all the deposits
　　　　　　Margravine of the trivia　　　　(Meander, Troy)
empress of the labyrinth
　　　　　　receive our prayers

　　　　　　laughing in the mantle of variety
　　　　　　belle of the mound
　　　　　　for lac o'-the Mound
　　our belle and annabelle
　　　　　　on all the world-mountain
In the December of our culture ward somewhere the secret seed under
the mountain, under and between, between the grids of the Ram's
survey when he squares the world-circle.

When the technicians manipulate the dead limits of our culture as
though it yet had life, have mercy on us. Open unto us, let us enter
a second time within your stola-folds in those days—ventricle and
refuge both hendref (= ancestral dwelling, winter quarters) for world-
winter, asylum from world-storm Womb of the Lamb, the spoiler of
the Ram.

The key to the Christian and very human view of David
Jones is the word "sacramental." He is far from the technopolis secular city of Harvey Cox, and though he no
doubt likes the vision of Teilhard de Chardin, especially
the *Divine Milieu,* he has no particular interest in the evolutionary theory of nature and mankind. He does, indeed,
suggest an alternative, one which I think can be extended
into an acceptable form of Christian humanism, which belongs to every age and culminates in the "recapitulation of
all things in Christ." The problem, which has no easy solution, consists in this: that the Christian way of life seems to
follow a quite different path from that of the secular ideal.

This was stated in the unforgettable contrast which St. Augustine made between the City of God and the City of Man. It is a language which puts Christianity into the same category as those high religions which regard the world as illusion or a place of misery or a Vanity Fair. Protestant and Catholic alike have preached this view, though Protestants are more suspicious of mystical prayer. Until recent times one might dare the generalization that all who meditated on human life and sought for a moral or spiritual perfection regarded the world as an obstacle to their aims. The classic work of à Kempis was a *vade mecum* in the nineteenth century and read by agnostics such as George Eliot.

Now this very general attitude toward the world could be maneuvered into an argument in favor of the modern change of mind. It was Bonhoeffer's exact point that man was so weak and ignorant in past ages that he naturally feared the world. He did not know how to manage it, or therefore to manage himself. Today he can embrace what he feared because he can make it an ally. This will do to explain a modification of the old view, but it leaves out the main reasons why there is and must be an antagonism of the sort mentioned between the City of God and the secular city. One can, besides, turn the tables on Bonhoeffer and say that ever since the Crucifixion—long before the twentieth century—God has in appearance left man to work alone and unaided by a special visible help from God. God, that is, has already retired behind the scenes. It is the silence of God which has always been a difficulty against the Christian belief. The cry of the Sunamite woman, "Did I desire a son of my Lord? Did I not say, do not deceive me?"—this cry has gone up generation after generation as the beloved one dies despite prayer and belief in the Providence of God. There is indeed a visible Church, but it is a sacramental presence, not the Christ who brought the son of the widow of Naim to life, and bade the waters of the lake be quiet. Before the death of Christ the presence of God seems to have been felt and enjoyed more than in the Christian era. God speaks to Moses and the prophets, He wakens Samuel from sleep, He terrifies Balaam, so over-whelms Ezekiel that he falls upon his face; He fills the holy Temple with glory. It is as if the people of God were more attuned to His nearness then than now, though in the Church is His real bodily presence. The rejection of Christ, not the twentieth century, is the decisive moment. God is exhibited once and for all as a mockery, as one "despised and rejected . . . And we hid our faces from him: he was despised and we esteemed him not." And so by the act of man God is hidden, no longer visibly operative, and man has had apparently to· rely upon his own resources. As Christ could have had legions of angels to help him in Gethsemane, but suffered, offering no resistance, so we, though we offer resistance, suffer alone.

This is part of the New Testament, God's providential economy; therefore it is not at all surprising that Bon-hoeffer should discover the truth even though so late in the day. But the corollary of Bonhoeffer that we must find God in our neighbor is only partly true. The old antagonisms have not been overcome—and this, too, was a discovery which St. Paul and the early Christians made. Christ had conquered the world, all now was orientated to Christ: he will show himself the Omega as well as the Alpha, and grace abounds. But though grace abounds the flesh still fights against the spirit, and the old vices of pride and ava-rice and self-indulgence torment man. We do not experi-ence the salvific presence of Christ, disposing of all things; we know the truth by faith but not by sight.

Hence the world has two meanings: one in which it is like the paradise in which Adam and Eve named the living creatures of God in joy and thereby grew in knowledge and love; secondly, the world in which the forces of evil are always seeming to triumph—a worldliness which is within the self and a worldliness in human relations, which manifests itself in feuds, cheating, oppression, brutality, vaulting ambition, and wars. What we mean by "the world" in this sense is "worldliness," the inability to live in it without sin private or public. It is this constant experience which gives the lie to those who would have the secular city the one place where religion now can be kept alive, and makes even P. Teilhard's view look Utopian. The secular city left to itself does become a Vanity Fair or something worse, and the growth of crime and the antinomianism of the young threaten to undo the very real virtues which are the genuine development of a long Christian tradition. Cox believes in material improvement, and by this means men and women will enjoy more leisure and have more opportunities of finding satisfaction in the arts. But the arts are in fact becoming more and more so specialized that there has been a return to primitive, if sophisticated, music and painting; and leisure of itself has never been creative unless it gives meditative moments to a mind meeting challenges and actively engaged. Leisure brings the boredom of idleness when there is no sense of vocation and no appeal like that, for instance, of a Peace Corps. Worst of all, in a city where God is not present, the citizens suffer a gradual suffocation, and after a while they lose the sense of who they are and what they ought to be about. It is, they say, against such a form of living—the whole modern society which Cox praises for its anonymity—that the Beatles and the hippies have revolted, if revolted be not too strong a term for the Arcadian or Paraguayan simplicity they seek. Nearer to them is John Clare:

> I left the little birds
> And sweet lowing of the herds,
> And couldn't find out words,
>   Do you see,
> To say to them goodbye
> Where the yellow cups do lie.

> So heaving a deep sigh
> Took to sea;

even though it was to an asylum he was taken.

The image of the Gospel is that of salt, and in those long past days the importance of salt in preserving food as well as giving it savor must have been greater than today, when there are so many sauces and the deep freeze can keep food eatable for so long. Christian ideals keep human life from going bad; like in that respect to a refrigerator: but this service is not a cold one nor a negative one. It is better to turn to another Gospel image—of the good soil in which the seed can live and grow. In such a soil the seed can not only grow, it can produce a miraculous crop. I have said that the earth is a sign and a sacrament, which means that it is both good and true in itself and also it tells of something beyond itself, as a city when it has an omphalos and a circle drawn around it became, so Mircea Eliade tells us, the center of the world, the spot where divinity dwells.

The best poetry and the best music possess this power of conveying some mystery beyond the words or the music. Helen of Troy can never again be just the stolen wife of a Greek prince; the cup I hold is more than the rough utensil bought at the shop; the signs of the Zodiac are not only constellations in the sky; above all, the fish reveals itself when it is spelled in the Greek, and the Cross across the ball of the universe alone makes sense of human living. For the full significance of this again it is well to turn to David Jones's poem *The Hunt*. How the old myths in so many tongues are summed up:

> when all the shining Arya   (nobles)
> rode with the diademed leader
> Who directs the toil
> Whose face is furrowed
> with the weight of the enterprise
> the lord of the conspicuous scars whose visage

with the hog-spittle whose cheeks are fretted with the
grime of the hunt-tool;
if his forehead is radiant
like the smooth hill in the lateral light
it is corrugated
like the defences of the hill
because of his care for the land
and for the men of the land

(His embroidered habit) is mired and rent and his
bruised limbs gleam from between the rents by reason of the
excessive fury of his riding when he rode the close thicket
as though it were an open launde . . .
for the thorns and flowers of the forest, the bright
elm-shoots and the twisted tanglewood of stamen and stem
clung and meshed him and starred him with variety
And the green tendrils gartered him and briary-loops
galloon him with splinter-spikes and broken blossom twining
his royal needlework

and ruby petal-points counter
the countless points of his wounds . . .

Here the whole landscape is the Christ and the whole
movement is his Passion. Here the beauty of nature finds a
new and perfect setting, as the Ghiberti bronze doors are
the opening to Christ's baptistery.

In the natural order life degenerates when there are no
resistances, and civilizations die out when they cannot meet
the challenge of changing conditions, new ideas or adversaries. The individual also succumbs to the world unless he
has built up within himself habits of virtue. Christianity,
however, seems to go beyond this because it encourages asceticism, the life of the monastery, and concentration on
heavenly things as opposed to earthly. It bids us at times
enter a Cloud of Unknowing and empty ourselves of all
that is creaturely so as to be filled with the Spirit of God.

Dr. K. Hughes, in his book *The Church in Early Irish Society*, quotes an early lyric:

> It were my mind's desire to behold the face of God,
> It were my mind's desire to live eternally with Him,
> It were my mind's desire to read books studiously,
> It were my mind's desire to live under a clear rule.

Now many texts in the Gospels and St. Paul do seem to demand a complete renunciation of earthly joys and ties, and the early Church insisted upon a severe discipline of unworldliness. St. Francis of Assisi at the end of his life said that he had been too hard on his body, which was also God's creature. Probably in the first centuries asceticism was regarded as essential for health, as bloodletting was the most common form of cure for illnesses. Again, bodily penance, fasting, and abstinence were supposed to alleviate carnal desires. But such reasons for penance do not explain why Christianity has stood for an ideal which looks at humanism with dubious eyes. As we have seen, some writers explain it by pointing out the misery of human life in past times, short lives, diseases abounding, injustice, and coarse appetites. Heaven in contrast was the golden city, where all tears would be wiped away; the stress too laid on the unregeneracy without grace of the human will, and the penances deserved because of sin. All this explains the past, and now that the world has become a livable home and man is master of himself, can the hard sayings of the Gospels be ignored?

The transition from the old spirituality to the new is explained by Fr. Ernest Larkin of the Carmelite Order.[10] He makes a contrast of the past and present attitude to the world. He begins by quoting from St. Teresa's *Interior Castle:* "When we empty ourselves of all that is creature and rid ourselves of it for the love of God, that same Lord

10 *Concilium,* vol. IX (London: Burks & Oates, 1967), pp. 52–57.

will fill our souls with himself." This he calls the spirituality of detachment in order to acquire charity, which is the
love of God for God's sake. It assumes a conflict within the
self. The authority for this assumption is to be found in
many places in the New Testament. One of them comes in
the seventh chapter of St. Paul's Letter to the Romans: "I
see another law in my members, warring against the law of
my mind, and bringing me into captivity to the law of sin
which is in my members. O wretched man that I am! who
shall deliver me from the body of this death? I thank God,
through Jesus Christ Our Lord." Here the language of St.
Paul is of struggle, of a war within oneself, which has to be
won by self-denial. By self-denial a disciple of Christ is
transformed into an *alter Christus,* and made ready for an
apostolate. In this ideal, Fr. Larkin says, "the Kingdom of
God is a kingdom of souls whose salvation is the 'one thing
necessary'" (the words of Christ to Martha about Mary),
the one absolute. All else is relative to this, no matter how
humanly attractive or important. The way of life, therefore, is one of detachment and purification, a putting off of
the old man and putting on the new. Purity of intention is
all important in a life which is a war between love of God
and inordinate self-love.

This view then, as just stated, obviously tends to neglect
the temporal and created order. The rival view makes up
for this neglect. In it we begin with the world and ourselves and expect to find God there. The Risen Christ lives
in the community, and as a consequence we must live fully
in the community. Our spirituality can in a new sense
(*vide* Bonhoeffer and Harvey Cox) be called worldly and
religionless. Instead of concerning ourselves so much with
sin and our own intentions and motivation, we should give
ourselves to works of positive charity, as objectively as possible and by direct confrontation. Such activity of itself
eases out sin and selfishness. We commit ourselves and become optimists relying on the promises of God. Mortifica-

tion need not be self-imposed, because the crosses of daily life which we meet will make us like to Christ. This view, Fr. Larkin says, is an offensive and looks forward, whereas the other view is a rearguard action. "The new asceticism teaches a way to God by extroversion and by action." It tends to neglect contemplation.

The sponsors of this more positive and optimistic view, as they claim it to be, also claim that they are in accord with modern humanism, modern spirituality in general, and with the spirit of the Vatican II Council. There has come to be a divorce between Christianity and modern society, and this cannot be right. Hence they are inclined to assign historical reasons—most of them no longer valid or potent—for what has happened. The divorce is an accident of time and not an essential separation. The world is now democratically minded. Of old imperialism was taken for granted, and so in religion all was for God and little or nothing for man. The Old Testament with its insistence— so needed in days of polytheism and anarchy—on the divine transcendence, omnipotence, and authority prevented the full change inherent in the New Testament from being realized. Then, too, the alliance of the Gospel with Greek thought was not entirely a blessing, inasmuch as the Greek underrated the function of the body in order to enhance the prerogatives and destiny of the spirit. This way of envisaging human life was crystallized by St. Augustine at a time when the Roman Empire was fading and a new Christian Europe was about to rise on its ashes. The great saints who followed taught after the manner of St. Augustine that the world was just a theater for the drama of salvation, and there over the horizon stood the city of peace, stable, everlasting, heavenly, invisible, and spiritual, and to it one passed through what was changing, transient, earthly, visible, and carnal. Aquinas, in turning his back on Plato to welcome Aristotle, was the precursor of a more human spirituality, and an opportunity came at the Renaissance for developing it. Man had then begun to find his place in the universe, but the excesses of the humanists and the need for an ascetic reform left the Church behind and led to the divorce which now exists. Such is the plea, and the modern attitude is well expressed by Robert Bultot in the same volume X of *Concilium:*

The emergence of the secular world as such, its unfolding according to its own internal laws, its claim to autonomy over against a Christendom that denied it and refused it, the proof it has given of the legitimacy of this claim by the undeniable value of so many achievements and ambitions, the purifying process it has imposed willy-nilly on religion and the Church—all this has forced theologians to become more fully aware of the object of redemption, to have a clearer idea of the concrete vastness of its scope and to take more serious account of texts that had been left on the fringe of their investigations.

Later he continues the argument, saying that we can no longer treat the history of salvation as if it were only a history of souls to be rescued from the wreck of creation: "what is saved is this creation itself." In agreement with this, J. Langmead Casserly writes that "the theme of theology is life and this life must be lived to the full as an inexhaustible source of joy before it can be interpreted theologically."

It would be easy to pick holes in the expression of this new view, but it is so positive and so much nearer to what we can believe of the generosity of God, that it must be accepted as a real contribution to Christian philosophy and theology. Where it needs modifying or correction is in its setting itself up over and against the old spirituality. The two must somehow be reconciled, because without question the Christian teaching contains the best in both views —as Christ himself in the ikons and old paintings held a ball representing the world and a scepter which we can interpret as a cross or crozier as well. *Regnavit a ligno Deus*— God reigning from a tree, a Cross of suffering. The demand for a reconciliation of the Cross and the world must not however rest on the argument that the Christian religion must be relevant to our modern society. This is a mean point of view, for it is society which has to find life, not the Church of God. Those who judge the worth of religion by its success forget that Christ himself failed utterly to win over his own people and was condemned by them and hung on a cross. It is this act of man in his initial encounter with God-made-visible which has to be taken into account in all genuine interpretation of Christianity and its relation to the world. The Crucifixion of a Loving God is so grave in itself and in its consequences that the second modern view, if made to substitute for the older view, becomes straightway suspect and so irreverent. The servant is not greater than his Master: and all optimists have to face the formidable, almost despairing cry of St. Paul after his failure in Athens: "I preach Christ crucified, to the Jews a stumbling block and to the Gentiles folly." It is only when that is said that optimism is justified "in the power and wisdom of God."

Those who fasten on the new spirituality without much reflection will, I fear, have a rude awakening. The surest way of dissipating the vigor of the Christian message is to hand it over to the secular arm, to trust human society without any qualification. This was the mistake made at the Renaissance, and in a small way by the worker priests in Paris. It can be called another case of Gresham's Law—the bad money driving out the good, or a debasing of the coinage. The solution, it cannot be repeated too often, must lie in some form of reconcilation between the two points of view. The modern one is very much needed to remove the harshness and at times zealotry, almost approaching to monomania, of the former view. It stressed overmuch the weakness of man, his proneness to sin, and the severity with which God judged his sin. Salvation did look, as the critics said, like the saving of a soul from the wreck. The body did look like a criminal deserving constant mortification. Human pursuits were in themselves vanity, profiting us nothing. They had somehow or other to be justified by some duty or unworldly purpose. The self was in jeopardy if it enjoyed itself even innocently. Augustus Hare tells of how his Victorian aunt made him, when a child, take some horrible medicine because he had accepted a chocolate biscuit when visiting friends. The ideal as taught in many spiritual books was to enjoy suffering humiliations or being neglected by others. Even to love friends, relations, parents, husband or wife or children was made difficult by the commandment to love God and to love him only.

Then there were the fearsome texts scattered about the New Testament, texts about giving up everything to follow Christ, as in the invitation to the rich young man, about taking up our cross daily, dying to self as the seed disappears in the ground, about hating mother and father and leaving them—"everyone that hath forsaken houses or brethren or sisters or father or mother or wife or children or lands for my name's sake shall receive a hundredfold . . ." St. Paul put these precepts and counsels into practice in his life, when he spoke of beating himself and of the multiple sufferings he took willingly upon himself or endured. It is strange at first reading to find the message of agapé, God's love for us and the world, conjoined with so many hard sayings. The truth must be—and the long, bloodstained story of man and his butchering of Love itself when God sent His beloved Son confirm it—that only by the tension created by the meeting of the ascetic and the human can man develop truly. Not only does the story of man confirm it, the experience of love makes it obvious. Love has in it always an element of self-sacrifice. Not only is the lover anxious to prove himself, but he becomes aware how poorly he loves and how coarse his love can be unless he draws upon all his resources to purify and elevate it. Marriages break up when the splendor of the vows grows dull and dim. The love of God, too, is unique. He does not enter into comparison with creatures. They are as naught compared with him, but, in order to realize this, poor man must shut his eyes to their attraction.

The relationship of love with God requires a special mode of sacrifice all its own. It is in God we live and have our being. From Him we come and to Him we return, "mote-like in God's mighty glow." As belonging to God completely our relation is realized even by the dullest to be unique. Nothing obviously can go right if this relation be askew, and then we see that it is not an easy matter at all to get the relation right: for God is invisible and His presence is not felt, and it is all too easy to slide into a life with closed windows and nothing but the bric-a-brac of our temporal occasions. The wise keep saying, "Put first things first," "Love God and all things will be added to you." But awaking glum and weary with various problems and anxieties to face, with the body playing us false and friends disappointing us, and routine hours and ephemeral excitements, we know only too well how much we would like to shake ourselves free and get the dormant prince in us to step onto the stage. From time immemorial the sages have advised man to choose times of silence and solitude, and to go in for some kind of spiritual exercises, be they Christian or yoga. The picture which the humanist and even the modern Christian writer has been drawing of human life is far too flattering. How strange it is that just when the Harvey Coxes, the Teilhard de Chardins, and many of the new school of Christians are telling us of the many excellences of the secular city or our evolving society, those who speak for that city or society are deploring the emptiness, even the nightmare quality of it. "The sun rose with no alternative on nothing new," as Samuel Beckett writes. We have besides Beckett, Ionesco labeled anarchist, Genet satanic; and from these wastes a poem is born. Bernard Buffet is the painter of "miserabilism." "Outside myself the universe is dolorous, hostile, dangerous. I think everyone must have this feeling." Of course by selection one can prove anything, but few would deny the sense of frustration which is so widespread, and shows itself not only in cultural circles, but also amongst the younger generation, whose habits and dress are so deliberately a protest against the secular city. As for the communist world, we have the sad declaration by Pasternak in *Dr. Zhivago:* "You and I are the last witnesses of all that immeasurable greatness which has been created in the world in all the thousands of years between them and us, and it is in memory of all those vanished wonders that we live and love and weep and cling to one another." One more piece of evidence to finish off this kind of critism of modern life. Ivan Valerin in *The Bluebottle* exposes the untruth in the belief that man is capable of achieving all the things his soul is yearning for by his own hands without, or even against, God. It is, he says of Russia, "an enormous hoax, a catastrophic piece of nonsense, a bluff on a world-wide scale." The result is "a faceless, furtive, cowardly horde of busy drones and ossified bureaucrats. If Communism is happiness for all, why are people so beastly to each other? And I remember in horror that I have never seen a happy man."

I quote this last passage because it dwells on the humanist dream of happiness, and speaks in the name not merely of the cultured but also the masses. Naturally humanists are inclined to think of happiness in terms of their own gifts, education, and culture, and they forget the vast numbers of men and women who would be lost in their Garden of Eden or the New Jerusalem of Harvey Cox. Those who live precariously in trade unions, in the docks, factories, and on the high seas, the simple folk who hardly read or write in India and China and South America, scrape happiness out of hardship and would be as out of place even in Teilhard de Chardin's supersociety as a squirrel in a cage. The miracle in human living is man's ability to make for himself heavenly moments even in a slum, and to look back with a touch of regret at life with others in a trench dugout or in a hospital ward. "The art of our necessities is strange, that can make vile things precious." All the more is this the case when suffering has a meaning and sacrifice is for a loved cause or friend. It would be difficult to think of any occupation, any game or pursuit, which has not an element of risk and strain, just as it is the hard test which calls out the best in a man and reveals him to himself.

I have called this the tension view of life as contrasted with the pragmatic one of our modern reformers and the evolutionary one of Teilhard de Chardin. Baron Friedrich von Hügel was the first I remember to call attention to the importance of this friction or salutary tension in explaining the mystery of man's endeavors and development. It is more diversified than the dialectic process, for the spur need not be antithetical. The hero or heroine who appeals to a child's imagination challenges without opposing youthful dreams and desires. Often enough, however, there is present that resistance or obstacle of which I have already written; but resistance can be subtly different. Men like Napoleon find their small size a challenge to become giants in power and authority, but it was not small size which has led President de Gaulle along similar lines.

The fundamental reason for the importance of tension is the division within ourselves and our own power to make a choice. Within ourselves the flesh fights against the spirit—in concupiscence and in the immediate attraction of sensation. Learning involves a battle against laziness and the pleasures provided by the senses, and holiness is a warfare against the protests of the body, of Eros against Agapé. The invisible always looks to be fighting a losing battle against the visible, and God to the modern school of theologians is turned into a name equivalent, and no more, to our neighbor. The true philosophy of tension, however, gives nothing away. It leaves us God, the ranks of spirits, man, and all that belongs to this world and to the starry heavens. They are not blanketed by a nominalist philosophy, nor left as a jigsaw puzzle which cannot be solved. Humanism without God is at its best like Lear in fortune and misfortune, "sunshine and rain at once: her smiles and tears." "Men must endure their going hence, even as their coming hither. Ripeness is all." But the obnoxious can ripen as well as the good, the scorpion and the rat, there is no fending off of death. At its less good, humanism turns Stoic or hedonist, and at its worst it hides its head in the sand. The religious truth is essential if we are to make sense of the world, make an order out of it, which is not imposed for our own purposes. Man can twist nature to his own purposes, but usually the result is unfortunate, and there is plenty of room for a modest pragmatism—and it may be essential for progress in certain departments of science. It is a grave mistake, all the same, to pretend that our human limitations mean also relativity in knowledge, and to translate the gradual appreciation of the world around us into a world without any contours or essences or values except those we give it. The knowledge of nature and life gives a humble joy as we come to see something of God's creation; and one criterion of truth here is its coherence and significance. The tension we feel is often between what we want to believe and do, and what is the one true and only answer. This is the long-drawn-out struggle between reason and rationalization, the truth about ourselves and our own loved image, between the love of others and the love of self.

On the human level, then, humanism cannot subsist without the assistance and the stimulus of religion. The animal in us is too strong if there be no divine authority to fear and love; and in the higher part of us the self ends up at best in an enlightened selfishness, if the intimations of another world are ignored. This is true on the natural level, and the exhortations and the denunciations of moralists and statesmen and sages throughout the ages prove the same. On the Christian level, the tension is far greater, as are the stakes; and where Christianity has penetrated, humanism without it looks like a blind and shrouded figure, by turns overconfident or grief-stricken. Christianity has been charged with neglecting the world in the pursuit of an invisible and perhaps incomprehensible ideal, of taking men and women away from their proper avocations to contemplate their navels or sit on top of pillars. Even Catholics now admit some truth in this accusation, and as we have seen, at times the world has been so brutal and subhuman that a Christian could not enter it without danger of sullying his soul. When St. Gregory Nazianzen of Cappadocia was appointed in the late half of the fourth century to the See of Constantinople, he wrote that there was no escape from "the maze of life: hated evil chains me to the ground; cares unlooked for buffet me on all sides, ravaging the grace and beauty of the soul." This was as much Platonic as Christian language, but Constantinople did have a poor reputation for morals. Still, such a sad cry as that of St. Gregory could find its echoes often enough, bearing witness to the difficulty of living a spotless life in large cities. The evil, however, is a matter of degree, and urban or rural life is the common lot of mankind. It is in order to make sure that the Church is not stifled in a city nor essentially hindered that Pope Paul VI has declared that "the Church is in the world, not of the world but for the world. . . . The Church does not prescind from this fundamental fact; that it is immersed in human society which, speaking existentially, precedes it, conditions it and nourishes it. . . . It [the Church] is mankind itself, lifted to a superior grade of new life."

It is this superior grade of new life which calls for a still greater tension in life, the firmest of resolves and loves, and a special, warm relation to men and things. This relation, without being explained, is the one indicated when Christ speaks of giving up all for the kingdom of God, and even hating mother and father. It is the same crisis of the self which makes some Christians leave the city for the mountaintop or suffer the pains of martyrdom. I have suggested that the clue to this paradoxical form of living is in the word "sacramental." But before this can be properly understood, the "new life" of which Pope Paul speaks must be understood. By the act of Christ our human life is lifted up into his, so that as he truly shared the divinity of the Father, so we identified in him also participate in the divine life. Now this is the highest form of love which is conceivable. Marriage is a symbol and a sacrament of it, because in marriage two become one as far as possible, and one spirit. In the sacrament of baptism we die to all that is unadaptable to the divine life, we cast our slough, "put off the old man," and in the symbolic act of immersion we die to rise a new kind of being, like to the Risen Christ. This (that is, the act of renunciation, dying to self, embodied in the hard sayings of the Gospel) is the preliminary to the full unity of the self with Christ which takes place in the sacrament and reality of the Eucharist. Then, going beyond the union of marriage, we become through Christ's body members of his body, new charged with his life, so that the Christian is Christ now here at this moment, in this place, and in the work he is doing, and in his meeting with his neighbor, who is now also closer to him than any natural relationship could bring about. The mystery is how we can both love the higher life of the Son of God Christ and remain contained within our own personality. But this is not a dark, forbidding mystery: it seems rather to belong to what supreme love might be able to achieve, though we do not understand how.

Here is the core of the Christian teaching, and it entails a special kind of humanism, where nothing finally is left out and all is seen in its original beauty and with a new grace. The paradox of Christian life is resolved in this way. As marriage means leaving one's mother and father for a new home, so a human being in being loved and chosen by God has to leave all to become one with Christ. This sundering in one sense is complete as one form of life is exchanged for another, and, as in marriage, the vows and complete commitment fit the occasion, so in the life of the Christian there must be a complete surrender of the self, love in action where the whole self is involved in the act of will. The spiritual life of self-denial, of detachment and of asceticism, follows on logically this initiation into the life of Christ, and as this has to be held to without retraction and increased all through life, the command to be ever vigilant and to take up the Cross stands to reason. Moreover, as this life grows most surely and steadily in putting on Christ, and the advent of the Son of God was to bring mankind into a unity with himself, a new kind of organism, if not species, it follows that the Christian life expands in loving relationships and in all the works of mercy.

This is where renunciation is made compatible with love of creatures and a life in the so-called secular city. Compared to the supreme act of dedication just described, all other loves are as nothing. That is to say, they are relative to this primal love, and there are times when the most bitter choices have to be made. But habitually the attitude to all that falls within the sequence of one's days is love raised to a new power. Everything glows with a new front. How this is so is described by Gerard Manley Hopkins in his spiritual notes: "Suppose God showed us in a vision the whole world enclosed first in a drop of water, allowing everything to be seen in its native colours: then the same in a drop of Christ's blood, by which everything whatever was turned to scarlet, keeping nevertheless mounted in the scarlet its own colour too." Everything speaks of God if we listen selflessly, but it is our own pragmatic interests which have not only interfered with admiration of beautiful objects for their own sake, whether natural or artifacts, but also with the simplicity of the vision which sees all things for what they are. With the initiation into the life of Christ (St. Paul also uses the analogy of adoption) comes a new way of seeing reality. It is described in terms of faith and hope and love. We see with new eyes because we begin to see with Christ's eyes, and that means with those of the operative Word of God, who made all things and gave them their intrinsic being and their password. Nature becomes far more precious and interesting, human beings are seen as brothers in Christ.

> And in his apparel of a poor man, and a pilgrim's likeness
> Many times God has been met, among needy people.

Closely knit into this faith-lit vision of man are hope and love; hope because of the power of Christ's victory over evil. Christianity is not only medicinal; it is a joy to the heart and a love letter from God, even to the tax gatherer, the prostitute, and the thief. Love finally consecrates and ordains all here and now and gives us an unfeigned and unadulterated sympathy with all that has been signed into creation by God.

Teilhard de Chardin contemplates a future when Christ will be as St. Paul says "all in all." The more surprising truth is that this happens in every generation and is going on now. The sacrament of the Eucharist transforms man now, and brings all nature under its shade, as the animals of the field gather under trees for coolness and refreshment from the pitiless sun. David Jones, as already shown, exploits with genius this truth of the sacramental character of life by showing the circumambience of all human cultural creations around Christ and specifically around the Eucharist. He argues that man is by nature a user of signs, for all he does is significant, and others understand these signs and their significance. But the signs can pile up, or rather roll around each other, suggesting a more and more universal theme and truth, as even the least act of making is typical of "that archetypal form-making" which is implicit in the words of the Christian creed, "by him all things were made." "None of us," says David Jones, "must allow ourselves to get away with the idea that we can avoid sacrament. To do so we should either have to suppose ourselves to be incorporeal intelligences or hippopotamuses or other such creatures of the Artifex, the Son. But try as he may no man can be like either of these, for along with his rational soul he has corporeality." Jones regards the natural world as complementary to Christ in his Revelation, for in the supposedly secular world are prefigurings, analogies, and coincidences which reach their full significance only in Christ. As a critic has said: "His funneling mind runs easily to analogy in this symmetrical universe of mirrors, finding like the Duke in *As You Like It,* books in the running brooks, sermons in stones." In this he resembles T. S. Eliot in his essay *Tradition and the Individual Talent.* David Jones goes further than Eliot in the exercise of his Christian imagination, but he would underline Eliot's words that "the poet must be aware that the mind of Europe, the mind of his own country—a mind which he learns in time to be much more important than his own private mind—is a mind which changes and that this change is a development which abandons nothing en route, which does not superannuate either Shakespeare or Homer or the rock drawing of the Magdalenian draughtsman."

Those who have followed the discussion in earlier chapters on the nature of development and of the relation of the pragmatic and relative to absolutes will see the relevance of Eliot's remarks to the whole question of an integral Christianity which remains at the same time faithful to its past, but ever ready to enrich its truth with the fresh information and cultural feeling of a new generation. It sees the world as sacramental and therefore as illustrating Revelation, and throwing more light upon it, as the plays of Shakespeare showed us as never before what man is like;

and, as the *Comedy* of Dante showed us man moving from the lowest to the highest so definitively, though the language is now obsolete and the *mise-en-scène* pre-Copernican. David Jones, as a believing Christian, sees many analogies in history and nature of the Christian mysteries, but his view at its simplest demands a relationship between man as an artist or artificer and God as Creator; so that no matter how much we try to be content with the secular it keeps on telling us of its sacramental character, "the intimate creatureliness of things, how trees are men walking, that words bind and loose material things." Here the secular is penetrated through and through with the sacred, so much so that to separate the secular from the sacred is like removing a flower from its natural bed and transferring it to a glass, where at best it can be kept artificially alive for a short while by replenishing the glass with water.

A secularism, then, without some kind of a religion is bound to be short-lived or look subhuman. That happened very quickly in Germany with Hitlerism. Owing to its very deep religious roots the dehumanization has been slower in Russia, and there is evidence to show that religion has never been successfully exterminated. The present-day irreligious humanist lives in the hope that he is strong enough to make a joyous world for himself without the help of the gods. They and the Christian secularists, who would compound together in one form of living the religious and the secularist, parade before us the forthcoming pleasures of such a life. Cox admires technopolis more than the Greek Christian admired Sancta Sophia: the filling station is more holy than the water stoup at a church entrance. Even P. Teilhard is smitten by the thought of a terrestrial paradise brought about by evolution where a higher species will dwell. But this seems to me an extraordinary romanticizing of human life as we know it.

At the moment I write there are headlines in the newspapers of an air disaster, in which nearly seventy lives are lost. Who does not feel a pang at such an end to many, young and old, and think of the agony of families and relations and friends? Sorrow is always near, for the more friends one has the more is one hurt in hearing of their illnesses and deaths and their disappointments—and they need not be friends. Books appear telling of the dreadful sufferings in Nazi concentration camps, and now we have equally sad stories, such as that of Eugenia Ginzburg, an innocent and devoted Russian teacher and journalist Communist, taken away from her husband and children and made to suffer a ruthless imprisonment for over twenty years, and all that without any proper trial or even hope of being judged fairly. No one who has an open heart and mind can live on indifferent to the sorrows of the world. And there are other griefs created by one's special situation, by the prejudices of class or color or country, by the misfortune of poor health or mental strain, by the decline of institutions and cities and countries one loves, and losses of faith. There are as well few signs of a decrease in petty jealousies, resentments, rivalries, and ingratitude. The marvel is how so many create a happiness for themselves and others in such conditions. One reason I have already given, namely, that of the challenge, which makes us more self-reliant and thankful for help in the crises of our life. But it is only when there is certain good news, and when an invitation to enjoy it is offered to us, that life takes on its full meaning, and a deep contentment can oust fear and the despondency due to the dark uncertainty of our fate.

The purely euphoristic ideal is not the Christian one— and such a humanism is a will-o'-the-wisp. The spiritual ideal will always be centered in a Cross, despite what some modern spiritual writers say. They are so fascinated by the new presentation of man, as grown up, as rid of fairy tales, as a demythologizer, as a custodian of a great new City of Man, that they bring their religious ideas into an accord with this new type of humanity. We are supposed to have crossed a border, where the rough and the smooth had to be equally endured and there was a never-ending struggle for existence. Now that that is over and all the world's peoples are close neighbors, there can be a smooth passage to a pleasant end. Religion must be as humane as the city: it should be relevant, helpful, no longer a policeman or oracle—no reminders of unworldly ideals, nor an irritating conscience. The aim of the religious man is to show how the humanist can be more human, even as the philosopher sees that the cups and saucers of the scientist are clean. Paul Lehmann (*Ethics in a Christian Context*) is quoted by Harvey Cox as suggesting that what God is doing in the world is politics; in other words, making and keeping human life human. Theology, for its part, Cox thinks, is a reflection-in-action, whereby "the Church finds out what the politician, God, is up to and moves in to work along with him." This syncopated version of a Christian humanism fails on many scores, as we have seen. It neglects the comprehensiveness of the Christian philosophy, the heavenly promises which are essential to it and embodied in its Creed, and lastly it leaves out the Cross.

The Christian faith cannot separate itself from the Cross. It is surprising that professing Christians can even suggest such a course. The orb or ball and the Cross make up the Christian coat of arms. Love as we know it on earth is almost synonymous with self-sacrifice. So close are they that many spiritual writers have mistakenly, I believe, identified them—teaching that love always chooses the harder. The reason for this is that the process of ridding oneself of selfishness involves a constant fight against the bias to look after "number one." Then, besides the fight against selfishness, there is the altruistic or centrifugal drive to give all to the beloved. When this beloved is God Himself, the Christ —and the giving of oneself means a new life in Christ—the emblem of the Cross becomes more and more significant. But this is not the end of the matter. The belief present from the beginning among Christians—to be found in the writings of St. Paul, the Petrine Letters, and the Fourth Gospel—is that God became man in order to reconcile man with God and bring all things into a new glorious order of which Christ was to be the head. This reconciliation was brought about by suffering and death endured at the hands of man, and therefore the Cross, the symbol of reconciliation, is the primary symbol of the Christian faith. The grim truth then is that man crucified God—rejected divine love, and revealed what an unregenerate and blind kind of creature man habitually is. He made for himself thereby a history which could not be one of paradisiacal union and peace. We can treat the rejection of Christ as a cosmic act, a representative choice of man, for according to the Bible account a people had been chosen out and given special commandments and directions; to them prophets had been sent who warned and adjured the leaders of the people. All this points to the importance of a choice to be made, which can be called cosmic, because though by Christ's coming the world was to be put right and kept safe in his hands, nevertheless the way this would work out under Providence was in the balance: salvation through the death of the Saving Lord or by acceptance of him. One can only conjecture what would have happened had the choice been one of acceptance. The prophets have provided us with great images, of the lion and the lamb at peace, but nothing concretely historical. One can say, I should think, that the differences between the sacred and the secular would not have been acute, if they could exist at all. Probably too the world would have grown really wise the more sophisticated it became, instead of deteriorating. The ugly fact in the way of our modern optimists is that whereas in ancient and more simple days concupiscence and the lust for power were the conspicuous vices, now it is the corruption of the mind—the philosophers fiddling like Nero while Rome is burning, the moralists making a virtue of disobedience, and the theologians putting God in a casket and cremating His ashes. Meanwhile *quicquid delirant reges plectuntur Achivi*—except that it is not kings who now rage and the Achivi are the suffering and despairing children of God. It is through this suffering that the image of the Son of God will revive, and it is by suffering, "even so as by fire," that all, in imitation of their Head, will win the victory and redress the world. They like Francis must bear the stigmata, "filling up what is wanting in the sufferings of a Christ" thorn-crowned, and so "bathe in his fall-gold mercies" and "breathe in his all-fire glances."

Christian optimism, therefore, has little sentimentalism in it, and does not rely on any naked efforts of man. It is confident that a Christian humanism is possible, and that there is no other abiding form. The alternatives turn subhuman or inhuman, after promising a brave new world. Christian humanism embraces soul and body, and comes alive in the new unity of Christ's risen body. Scriptural scholars and theologians agree more and more in the view that what is called the Body of Christ or "the Mystical Body" is not just a symbol or a spiritual union. St. Paul, with his Hebrew background, wrote realistically of the actual Body of Christ risen from the dead. It is by his body that we are incorporated into Christ, and thereby as he is one with the Father and the Spirit we are sanctified by the Spirit—the link of love in the mystery of the Trinity. How this can be is beyond our understanding; but there are analogies in the Trinity itself, and in the unifying act of a consummated marriage, and the means we know, the lifegiving means, which is the Eucharist, the Shekinah, and real presence of Christ. Human beings feeding on Christ are lifted up into a higher form—not a new species, but a form of divinization in a God-man wherein they remain intensely human. What is dissolved is the self-centered life, the individuality which forms a barrier between one man and another. Always men are striving to overcome their loneliness by associations, deep friendships, family, and other forms of togetherness. There is always an intimation —but never realized—of a still higher union; and the fact that human beings can in some mysterious way substitute for others and take on their burdens shows that this higher union may not be just a dream—no more than the love expressed, for instance, in *The Phoenix and the Turtle* ("Each shall be both, yet both but one"), or by a throng of mystics. "Not this," so many have cried of a mortal union, "not this the soul's desire." There are such surprises in nature of the power and extent of certain forces that the possibility cannot be ruled out of a supercharged body, which would pass on its own vitality and create a resemblance of itself in another body. The problem arises not only in connection with the Risen Body of Christ, but with the resurrection of each body as taught in the Creed. Here it would seem as if the spirit could be so personal that, owing to an indissoluble tendency to materialize itself, it would always in some way be making a body for itself, as a magnet attaches alien objects to itself. This would help to explain the fairly well attested evidence of apparitions of the dead in bodily form or even, what is again attested, bilocation. If by belonging to the Body of Christ we are never just a spirit, strengthless or strong, then what has been suggested of the natural power of the spirit to embody itself would serve as a preparation for a higher form of union.

The famous passage of St. Paul on the place and function of Christ in forming and constituting a new humanity fits in, with reservations, with the views of Teilhard de Chardin; they also give Scriptural warrant, an even better warrant, to a humanistic ideal where Christ through our incorporation in him will be finally revealed as the Alpha and the Omega, not of a superorganism, but of his new Body, human but divinized: a group feasting, a city, a kingdom, a new earth and a new heaven, for "in Christ all created things took their being, heavenly and earthly, visible and

tion of society within a single rational system. This is an important point both in itself and as leading on to his theory of wholeness or unity and metacriticism. There will come about in the new society a continuing cycle of enquiry and feedback, and this will culminate not in facts but in images; and these "images" can form the basis of a rational system of control in which particular points of view are absent or at any rate neutralized. In this system we displace the ultimacy of individual self-consciousness and free choice—and all comes about inevitably as the old cult is overthrown (I am not sure whether Richardson is discarding the value of the self or raising it to a higher level in some new whole as Teilhard de Chardin tries to do). His evidence here again is somewhat unconvincing. He says that the Protestant with his belief in individual experience of God may be shocked, but the Biblical view of history was due to a limited conception of time and space, and the Protestant emphasis on personal self-consciousness was a mere projection of eighteenth-century philosophy into history. Now, "Just as the personal God of the modern intellectus undergirded the ultimate value of individuals, so the God of the sociotechnomic system of the world must be reconceived as the unity of the manifold system of the world." God is to be the "unity of community." This he calls the American way of thought and life. It is American Christians who have appreciated the work of the Holy Spirit. For them God is a social system within which individuals have their part. The system works not by precise thought forms, but pragmatically, and individual morality must be taken up into a set of social principles bearing on teamwork, conformity, and organization. Here he draws near to Harvey Cox, but, as we shall see, he is far more metaphysical, and he makes distinctions within secularism.

In fact, he distinguishes five forms of secularism varying according to the cult prevailing at the time. I do not think Richardson is a very safe guide in history, and so I confine myself to his description of the present relation of faith to society and its way of living. He thinks there is a reconciliation going on. The relative character of all social judgments needs a kind of faith which is an "opening out to a transcendently redemptive reality." Faith now seeks to unite the many relative perspectives and prevent conflict from arising from racialism and segregation and other ideologies. In other words, there is a need, besides the discipline of sociology, of a metacriticism, and he adapts a saying of Marshall McLuhan that "the myth is the message." Myth serves to unite the multiple experience of modern man, and myth depends upon what he calls "feeling"—not just a feeling, for example, of pain or excitement, but what makes us participate in what is perceived and feel it as a whole. This feeling of wholeness is gathered up in the myth. This "wholeness" is joined to a "feeling of rightness or fittingness, and again of well-being and happiness." In religious experience, above all, "participation" is felt; we make "contact with the All Encompassing Whole," and have "a sense of the Glory of the Divine Being" (Jonathan Edwards). This participation, which precedes all words, requires imaging forth, and for this reason "myths and images are needed to undergird the experience." "Myths are images used in religion," and he assumes that images symbolize wholes; they participate in the reality they express and are irreplaceable. Here the medium is the message. Richardson then insists that besides truths which depend on correspondence or consistency and are rational, there is a mystical truth which consists in the "evocation of the feelings of wholeness, rightness and well-being."

On this a metaphysic can be built, and Richardson tries to do it, calling the result a "philosophy of unity." The multiple sciences and modern modes of experience demand this meta-discipline as a unifying principle. What management now constitutes in the institutional and practical order, this kind of theology will serve as "the principle of all methodological possibilities." I wish I could praise what now follows, but I find it difficult to make good sense of it. He argues that "the being [existence] of a thing is its unity," and this unity is not the same as "essence, which, as explained, characterizes various objects." In statements like these Richardson seems to me to be misusing old settled terms difficult enough in themselves but carefully separated, and to make complete confusion out of them. He tells us essences may well be different, but they all have unity—each having a special unity. There is the unity of a determinate essence which gives it its identity, the "that whatness," which is irreducible oneness, distinguishing it from other realities and from nothingness. Hence essence and existence are not two separate objects, for existence is nothing other than the unity which we call identity. As Richardson spends many pages trying to express what he means, any brief account may be unfair; but I cannot believe that any real, worthwhile information has been given to us in saying that essence and existence are not two separate objects (as if either by itself could be an "object"!) and that existence, unity, and identity are all the same.

He does, however, distinguish three kinds of identity: individuality, relationship, wholeness. (How relationship, which by its very nature must refer to at least two related objects, can stand by itself, I do not know.) Aristotle made substance the matrix of all the other divisions. Richardson rejects this for the very odd reason that a relation is just as one as an individual or substance. He prefers "relationship" as matrix because he thinks that it would make intelligible such concepts as space-time and empty space, and individuals could be described as "rational intersections." For these and other reasons he chooses "the unity of wholeness." Then Omnipotence would be a whole as archetype and as fully present in all the parts "as America is in every part of it; and so we could say truly that Jesus Christ was present in all the world." It is remarkable how Richardson hacks his way through what seemed an impenetrable forest of abstract words to an idea of metaphysical and religious unity and wholeness, which he believes fits the form of Christianity natural to Americans. We can talk truth, he says, on three levels—sensible experience, scientific, and philosophical—and they can be united in "a unity of the unities." A simple knowledge of steel, for instance, as individual can then grow as it is contained within a scientific account, and then within the relational system which embraces all reality. To account for all these separate unities, "we must affirm not only the reality of the three unities . . . but also the reality of the Unity of the Unities." "Hear, O Israel, the Lord, our God: the Lord is One" (Deut. 6:4).

In the last part of his book Richardson comes down to earth—the land of the United States. The Reformation, he tells us, was excessively identified with, if not a product of, the social and economic unrest of the time. So religion could not have a fair chance till Christianity was established in America. In the traditional Western interpretation of Christianity, there are noticeable defects, such as the disproportionate emphasis on the New Testament and especially St. Paul. Sin is made too central and has, as a result, distorted the nature of Christ's work. God's intention in creating the world has been neglected, as well as the place of the Trinity in life and that of the Holy Spirit in communal life. The American genius has revealed Christianity as a holy worldliness and a sanctification of all things by the Holy Spirit. The emphasis given by the Puritans to the Sabbath is picked out as a mark of the purest Christian truth. Man is made for Sabbath holiness, for his end is not in himself but in the holiness of God, which, by means of the Sabbath, is established in the world as the final joy of all created things. It is American Christianity which asks why did God create the world, and the answer lies in the old Puritan formula: "The chief end of man is to glorify

God and to enjoy Him for ever." Hence the reason why God created the world is the Sabbath. Here is God's glory, and holiness and glory go together, for neither Otto nor Tillich fully grasped the significance of God's holiness. It refers to God's dignity, and it is by His dignity that God surpasses all else.

In the light of this, Richardson regards it as a mistake to begin with Christology or the Cross. The "theology of the Cross can actually be shown to be a Western accommodation to Arianism and naturalism." The connection of the Incarnation with sin has been exaggerated. "The Sabbath day was created by God so that He himself might enter into the world and sanctify it by His personal presence." Again, the Western world impregnated with Hellenism has invented bad formulas such as that of the God-man. Such a division makes God's nature or essence incapable of being in the world, and so God is said to be beyond or above it. This makes it impossible to regard the humanity of Christ as essential to God's own being. In truth the world is holy with God's holiness, and "in this sense holiness is ascribed to the world irrevocably and not just analogically." Also, "just as Jesus Christ is an uncreated person who unites in himself both divine and human nature, so the Holy Spirit is an uncreated person who unites in Himself both another divine person and a human person." It is American Christianity which makes clear the personality of the Holy Spirit, and it is here in this theology of the Trinity that American Christianity shows itself "no less unique and important than either the Reformation Protestantism or Roman Catholicism." The old kind of redemptive theology failed to give reasons for the divinity and work of the Holy Spirit. It was too concerned with sin and the sixth day. The Holy Spirit's work is for God's glory and for the presence of His holiness. "The Spirit creates no higher life with better faculties, no special visions or charisms, no extramental or extramoral consciousness." He is the Spirit of Sabbath holiness, and that is enough.

Why does Richardson call this view especially American? He answers that its primary themes are found only in America. "Where else has the Sabbath been a major doctrinal theme?" Again, alone American theology asks what was God's intention in creating the world, and explains it adequately, for Richardson can fit it in with "the positive American attitude towards technology, the instrument whereby man transforms his world." Here at last sanctification replaces the old redemptive view. Richardson sees in the constant use by Americans of psychotherapy, technology, social reform, and political action adjuncts to the Gospel, whereas in Europe they are feared.

This then is a courageous attempt to give a modern, positive reconstruction to the Gospel message. There is no objection to trying to reformulate that message so long as the divine message comes through the formulation unmutilated. It is difficult to be sure what Richardson thinks to be primary or essential in the divine message. He seems at the end to rule out the supernatural, and I do not know whether he accepts a kingdom which is not of this world. So far as I can follow his distinctions of divinity and humanity in Christ, he ties divinity to what is human and ends by destroying any distinction. If Christ's humanity is essential to his divinity and to the Second Person, it must exist before that creation of the world which Richardson admits. The metaphysical account with its attempt to make so much of the notion of unity ends, I fear, in saying nothing at all. A unity is always of something and is intelligible only in terms of what it unifies. Apples make a unity— apples in a barrel another; a regiment which has existed two hundred years has a unity; a house has a unity, so too a state, and the Mystical Body of Christ. At the beginning he said the epoch of personalism and self-consciousness and choice was over; yet at the end he is struggling to allow for the personality of the Holy Spirit. The way he began to develop his metaphysic seemed inevitably to lead to a kind of anonymous pantheism where the Unity of Unities would take the place of a triune God. I have already expressed distrust of his history. Richardson does not seem to be aware of the place of the Holy Spirit in Eastern Orthodoxy and the Uniat Churches, nor of the constant belief in the glory of God as the end of creation in Western liturgy and spirituality. The Mass begins with a *Gloria* and at its climax before the *Pater Noster* glorifies God in and through and with Christ. The famous *Exercises* of St. Ignatius begin with the statement that man's end is to glorify God, and the common Penny Catechism says the same.

This same disregard of the teaching in the Western tradition is almost palpable in Richardson's remarks on American spirituality and mysticism. It is as if Jonathan Edwards alone had had mystical experience. Let Richardson read Juliana of Norwich or *The Cloud of Unknowing*, and then turn to the great mystics of the Low Countries and Spain. He dismisses European theology as too concerned with Christology and sin. In this as in many other places in his book, he shows an original insight, but it is then spoiled by exaggeration—or can it be by lack of knowledge? There may have been in the past a preoccupation with sin and death and judgment, an interest which produced dark, magnificent poems like the *Dies Irae*. Theologians have for the most part treated the Redemption as the reconciliation of sinning man through Christ with the Father. But the Franciscans and others used the great Pauline conception of all creation centering around Christ. What Richardson thinks to be so novel and American is in Robert Grosseteste, *circa* A.D. 1230: "The Incarnation would have happened even if man had never sinned: it was necessary to complete man's natural glory. Since human nature is capable of union with God, God must have from the beginning intended to crown man's natural endowments by sharing His nature. In this act creation was completed." This view is in Duns Scotus and in many other writers. Even I, in *The Meaning and Matter of History,* tried to develop the theme in a contemporary way.

I do not see, therefore, why Richardson should be so anxious to make old themes sound new and American. It seems to me that the best in American spirituality should continue to develop the great inheritance of West and East, like a good householder who brings out treasures both new and old. The glory of God and His Christ cannot be dimmed in some secular city, nor by ignoring the past. Please God American Christianity will show a new facet of the abiding truth, and I hope Mr. Richardson may contribute.

APPENDIX 2

The ideas in the text were thought out before the official decrees of the Second Vatican Council were published. In *The Documents of Vatican II,* as edited by Walter M. Abbott, there are many passages which touch on the problems of Church and State, Christianity and secularism. I transcribe here two or three passages which may induce readers to read for themselves the whole of the *Pastoral Constitution of the Church in the Modern World.*

After stating that the new conditions of life facilitate a "more critical ability to distinguish religion from a magical view of the world and from the superstitions that still circulate, which purifies religion and exacts day by day a more personal and explicit adherence to faith" (p. 205), the Pastoral goes on to say that "as a result many persona are achieving a more vivid sense of God; on the other hand, growing numbers of people are abandoning religion in practice. Unlike former days, the denial of God or of religion or the abandonment of them are no longer unusual and individual occurrences. For today it is not rare for such decisions to be presented as requirements of scientific progress or of a certain new humanism. In numerous places these views are voiced not only in the teachings of philosophers, but on every side they influence literature, the arts, the interpretation of the humanities and of history, and civil laws themselves" (p. 205).

Later on we read that "the living conditions of modern man have been so profoundly changed in their social and cultural dimensions that we can speak of a new age in human history" (p. 260). "Little by little a more universal form of human culture is developing, one which will promote and express the unity of the human race to the degree that it preserves the particular features of the different cultures. In every group or nation there is an ever-increasing number of men and women who are conscious that they themselves are the artisans and authors of the culture of their community. Throughout the world there is a similar growth in the combined sense of independence and responsibility. Such a development is of paramount importance for the spiritual and moral maturity of the human race. . . . Thus we are witnesses of the birth of a new humanism."

In the face of this new humanism we are told that "Christians on pilgrimage towards the heavenly city should seek and savour the things which are above. This in no way decreases but rather increases the weight of their obligation to work with all men in constructing a more human world." This can be done because the Christian faith provides excellent incentives to doing energetically and perfectly the work lying before each person, for "manifested at the beginning of time, the divine plan is that man should subdue the earth, bring creation to perfection and develop himself." "No doubt today's progress in science and technology can foster a certain exclusive emphasis on observable data, and an agnosticism about everything else." Such a result does not necessarily follow, and its danger should not "lead us into the temptation of not acknowledging its positive values. For among its values are these: scientific study and strict fidelity towards truth in scientific research, the necessity of working together with others in technical groups, a sense of international solidarity, an ever clearer awareness of the responsibility of experts to aid men and even to protect them, the desire to make the conditions of life more favourable for all, especially for those who are deprived of the opportunity to exercise responsibility or who are culturally poor. All of these values can provide some preparation for the acceptance of the message of the Gospel, a preparation which can be animated with divine love by Him who came to save the world" (p. 262).

On a later page we read about the two cities or spheres, "in their proper spheres, the political community and the Church are mutually independent and self-governing. Yet by a different title, each serves the personal and social vocation of the same human beings. This service can be more effectively rendered for the good of all if each works better for wholesome mutual co-operation, depending on the circumstances of time and place. For man is not restricted to the temporal sphere. *While living in history he fully maintains his eternal vocation* [my italics]. The Church founded on the Redeemer's love, contributes to the wider application of justice and charity within and between nations. . . . There are, indeed, close links between earthly affairs and those aspects of man's condition which transcend this world. The Church herself employs the things of time to the degree that her own proper mission demands. . . . Holding faithfully to the Gospel and exercising her mission to the world, the Church consolidates peace among men, to God's glory. For it is her task to uncover, cherish and ennoble all that is true, good and beautiful in the human community" (p. 288).

INDEX

Birth control, moral question of, 97, 138–39

Blackham, H. J., 4, 6

Blake, William, 37

Blondel, Maurice, 101

Bloomsbury group, 73

Bluebottle, The (Valerin), 188

Body: and its functions, prejudice against, 113; and presence of reality around us, 125–26

Bonaventure, St., 64, 203

Bonhoeffer, Dietrich, 2, 55, 82–83, 86, 165, 176, 177, 182

Bossuet, Jacques Bénigne, 143

Botticelli, Sandro, 123

Brabham, H. J., 55–56

Bracton, Henry de, 50

Brave New World (Huxley), 70

Breboeuf, Jean de, 103

Buber, Martin, 12, 93

Buddha, 45

Buffet, Bernard, 187

Bultmann, Rudolf, 55

Bultot, Robert, 184

Burnham, James, 69

Campbell, Roy, 132

Camus, Albert, 23, 95

Cannibalism in Fiji, 98

Capote, Truman, 165

Casserly, J. Langmead, 184

Certainty, 5, 31–40, 75–76, 79, 107, 108–10, 117; absolute and relative, 132–33; physical, 132–133; moral, 132, 133–34

Certitude, antipathy toward, 4

Cerveau, Michel de, *see* de Cerveau, Michel

Challenge: developmental need of, 71–72, 197; of the secular city, 87; of changing conditions, 180

Chardin, Teilhard de, *see* de Chardin, Teilhard

Chaucer, Geoffrey, 169

Chiang Yee, xix*n.*

Chichester, Francis, 68

Chinese ideograph, symbol of humanism, xviii–xix

Christian faith, and the Cross, 198–200

Christian humanism, *see* Humanism, Christian

Christian optimism, 200

Christian Pavilion at Expo '67, Montreal, 170

Christian saints, practices of, 63–64

Christian spirituality, 155, 162–163; *see also* Spirituality

Christian theology of past, 86

Christian view of life, 164–202

Christian way of life and that of secular world, intercourse between, 171–72

Christianity: history of, 46–53; and humanism of Middle Ages, 48–52; *rapprochement* of, with secular society, 54, 107; future of, in identification with secular city, 85, 113; and modern life, reconstitution together of, 91–92; import of, in modern urban life, 92; problem of, in relation to secular life, 94; brought up to date, 95; connection today with its past, 97; importance of history in estimate of, 112–14, 143; fraternizing of, 143–63; as a truly historical religion, 146; and the world, making peace between, 147; traditional, ideals promoted by, 167; and modern society, divorce between, 183–184; in America, 207–9, 210–11

Christologie et Évolution (de Chardin), 163

Chrysostom, John, 115, 150

Church: first fruits of liaison with world, 47; corruption of, 52–53; period of reform in, 53; attitudes of, to modern society, 54; and State, contest between, 55; failure of, to command attention of modern generation, 65–66; place of, in the world, 191

Church in Early Irish Society, The (Hughes), 181

City of God: defiled by City of Man, 52; and City of Man, St. Augustine's division between, 82, 113, 176; and City of Man, making peace between, 147, 162; reconciling of, with secular city, 153

City of God (St. Augustine), 47

Clare, John, 178

Classicism: change from, to historical consciousness, 14–15, 16, 107, 108, 109; and "static" truth, 108

Claver, Peter, 103

Codes and laws of human behavior, 42–43

Collingwood, R. G., 40

Comment Je Crois (de Chardin), 160

Commission to Study the Organization for Peace, 59–60

Communism, 66–67, 69–73, 98, 188, 203; and Western civilization, widening antagonism of, 159

Conaesthesia, 125–126

Conceptual scheme, and reality, 38

Consciousness: religion as deeply inset in, 44–45; harmonized collectivity of, 150; technological simulation of, 168

Conservatism, 69

Constable, John, landscapes of, 123

Contemplation on Divine Love, 161

Convergence in nature toward unity, 157n.

Converging society, theory of, 170

Cosmic Christ, 149, 152, 153

Cosmos, history of, as history of divinization, 161

Council of Trent, 52, 110

Cox, Harvey, 8, 51n., 85–105, 106, 107, 113, 132, 134, 159–60, 164–165, 166, 168, 170, 173, 175, 178, 182, 188, 196, 198, 204

Crea, Pierre Reginald, 160n.

Crime, growth of, 164, 178

Critiques (Kant), 130

Croce, Benedetto, 40

Crusades, 102, 115

Cult, crisis of, 203

Culture: post-Christian, 83, 167; of definitions, 107; relativism in, 107; and spiritual movements, 115, 117; Western, 128

Luke, St., 103
Luther, Martin, 27

Maetzu, Ramiro de, 69
Maitland, F. W., 50
Man, Function and Society (Maetzu), 69
"Man has come of age," 2, 82; and existentialism, 8
Managerial Society (Burnham), 69
Marcel, Gabriel, 9, 11–12, 21, 23
Marcus Aurelius, 46
Maréchal, 122
Maritain, Jacques, 53, 122, 149, 151–53, 161
Marlé, R., 144, 145
Martin, Kingsley, 4n., 5–6, 57
Marx, Karl, 27, 42, 44, 49, 70, 72, 73, 171
Marxist philosophy, 3, 23, 27, 44, 49, 52, 67, 68, 69–73, 113
Material prosperity and contentment of soul, contrast between, 166
Materialsm, 52, 70, 150
Maturity of man, *see* "Man has come of age"
McLuhan, Marshall, 2, 167–70, 205
Meaning of the Death of God, The (Shideler), 84
Meaning and Matter of History, The (Anshen), 210
Meaninglessness of life, fear of, 60–61
Medawar, Peter, 37, 156, 161
Megalopolis, 170, 174
Mentoid, 156

Merleau-Ponty, Maurice, 36
Metanoia (repentance), 90
Metaphysics, 24, 31, 89, 124
Middle Ages, humanism of, 48–52
Mind, latent in every particle of matter, 156
"Miserabilism," 187
Missionary movement of nineteenth century, 102
Mobility: and the secular city, 87, 88; of early Christians, 102
Modern civilization described, 2
Montaigne, Michel de, 115
Montesquieu, 115
Moore, G. E., 73
Moral decisions and act of faith, comparison between, 109
Moral obligation to help others achieve happiness, 57, 58
Moral Rearmament, 167
Morality: and needs of civilized society, 6; basic structure of, 14, 38–39, 97; and results of morally good actions, 78–80; relativity of, 97–98
More, Thomas, 44, 115
Morlaix, Bernard de, 89n.
Morris, William, 92
Moses, 103, 177
Murray, John Courtney, 107, 108–9
Mussolini, Benito, 69
Mystical view of life, 81n.

Names given God, 92, 93, 96–97, 99–100
Nationalism, growth of, 52
Natural law, and moralists, 14
Natural order of man, 51

Prosperity, material, and contentment of soul, contrast between, 166
Proudhon, Pierre Joseph, 102
Proust, Marcel, 66, 127
Pythagoras, 78

Rahner, Karl, 26, 34, 107, 135–138, 142, 159
Rationalism, 3, 5, 23, 55, 81
Ravier, André, 150
Reactionaries, The (Harrison), 23*n.*
Reading, ousting of, by electronic devices, 167
Reality, 37–38, 122, 123, 124, 126, 135, 194; historical, 91
Reason: playing down of, 7; pre-eminence of, 30–31, 143; and humanism, 41; and rationalization, struggle between, 190
Recapitulation of all things in Christ, 175–76
Reformation, 27, 52
Religion: and Marxist philosophy, 3, 23, 44, 49; and humanism, 43–81, 85, 190–91; supernatural, and contest with secularism, 55; growing indifference to, in today's world, 64–66, 82; and communism, 66–67; bringing up to date, 85; and economy, correlation between, 85–86, 113–14; effects of, in political sphere, 105; present crisis as reflection of changes in history, 117–18; and science, reconciliation between, 155–59

Religion in Modern Society (Brabham), 55–56
Religious thought, history of, 26–28
Religious truths: and history, intimate connection between, 144; and making order out of world, 190
Renaissance, 2–3, 9, 52, 183
Republic (Plato), 78
Reuther, Walter, 93
Revelation, 140, 145–46, 195
Revolution, industrial, x
Richardson, Herbert W., 202–11
Ricks, Christopher, 169
Robinson, J. A., 55, 85, 102
Rock and the River, The (Thornton), 8–9
Roman Empire, decline of, 47, 82, 183
Rousselot, P., 122, 123–24
Ruskin, John, 127
Russell, Bertrand, 4*n.*, 33, 55, 58, 73, 81*n.*, 114, 119*n.*
Ryle, Gilbert, 4*n.*

Sacramental form of living, 192, 194–95
Sacramental value of all created things, 171, 173
Saints, Christian, practices of, 63–64
Samuel, 177
Sanctifying grace, Church's doctrine of, 154
Sanders, N. K., 172–73
Sartre, Jean-Paul, 9, 11, 12, 19–20, 21, 23, 29, 95
Schopenhauer, Arthur, 56

Schweitzer, Albert, 61
Science and religion, reconciliation between, 155–59
Scientific Humanism (Southern), 49
Scientific humanism, failure of, x–xi
Scientists of today, 3–4
Scott, Walter, 66
Second Vatican Council, 52, 104, 183, 212–14
Secular city, 82–105, 106; growing strength of, 82; identification of Christianity with, 85, 113; challenge of, 87; and mobility, 87, 88; reconciling City of God with, 153
Secular City, The (Cox), 51*n.*, 85, 92, 94, 101, 104, 106, 159
Secular humanism, *see* Humanism, secular
Secularism, 55, 82, 196, 212
Secularist society, *rapprochement* of Christianity with, 54, 107
Secularization, distinguished from secularism as ideology, 90
Self-consciousness, intensification of, 131
Self-interest, enlightened, 79
Self-knowledge, 122, 123
Self-sacrifice, and love, 186
Self-sufficiency of man, high degree of, 165
Self, wordliness within, 177–78
Seneca, 46
Shideler, Emerson W., 84
Simeon Stylites, St., 62
Sociotechnics, new cult of, 203–4
Socrates, 16, 78, 107, 115, 128
Sohn, Louis, 59

Soul of the world, 151
Southern, R. W., 49
Spatial supernatural world, 102, 103
Spencer, Herbert, 149
Spinoza, Baruch, 17
Spiritual athleticism, 53
Spiritual Exercises, The (St. Ignatius of Loyola), 161, 210
Spiritual language, and changes in society, 116
Spiritual poverty, approval of, 115–16
Spirituality: 155, 162–63; transition from old to new, 181–83, 184, 185; of detachment, 182, 193; modern, 183, 185; American, 210, 211
Static truths, and humanism, 41
Stoics, 14, 45–46, 74, 190
Strachey, Lytton, 73
Strawson, P. F., 37–38
Suetonius, 47
Supernatural order of man, 50–51
Survival of fittest, and evolution, 71
Suttee in India, 98
Sweeney, Leo, 21

Tacitus, 47
Technopolis, 2, 89, 90, 91, 92, 93, 95, 99, 104, 173, 175; *see also* Secular city
Teilhard de Chardin, *see* de Chardin, Teilhard
Tennyson, Alfred, 137
Tension view of life, 27, 189–90, 191–92
Teresa of Avila, St., 64, 117, 181

Theism: and existentialism, 11; and pragmatic thought of today, 13

Theology: revolutionary features of, 90; and the urban secular man, 94–95; and history of meaning of words, 110–12; and contemporary culture, 120–21; and neglect of factor of time and history, 129; and dogma, 145; of the Cross, 208

Thomas à Kempis, 143, 176

Thomas Aquinas, St., 11, 17, 27, 49, 89, 101, 121, 129, 130, 157, 183

Thomistic philosophy, 17

Thornton, Martyn, 8–9, 119n.

Thought and Action (Hampshire), 37

Tillich, Paul Johannes, 55, 208

Tolstoy, Leo, 66

Towards an American Theology (Richardson), 202

Tractatus Logico-Philosophicus (Wittgenstein), 4n.

Tradition and the Individual Talent (Eliot), 195

Tresmontant, Claude, 152

Truth, objective, 15–16; 101, 108

Truths: change in outlook and in insight into certain types of, 16–17; static and dynamic, 16, 23, 26, 38, 40, 118–20, 132, 133, 138, 141, 143; contemporary dislike of immobility in, 39–40; versions of, 121–23; general relativity of, 132; coherence view of, 136–37; doc-

trinal and moral, 138–39; religious, 140–41

Two cities: theory of, 94, 106–42; problem of, and humanism, 118

Tyndall, John, 157

Unifying action of divine Presence in world, 161

Unity of Indirect Reference, 34–35

Unity, philosophy of, 205–7, 209

Unworldliness, insistence of early Church on, 181

Vahanian, Gabriel, 83

Valensin, A., 122

Valerin, Ivan, 188

Values, relativization of, 87, 98

Vatican Council, Second, 52, 104, 183, 212–14

Vico, Giambattista, 115

Vinogradoff, Paul, 50

War, moral question of, 97

Wilberforce, Samuel, 147

Wilder, Amos, 92

Willis, Lord, 56

Wittgenstein, Ludwig, 4n., 127, 156n.

Woolf, Leonard, 73

Woolf, Virginia, 72, 73

World: becoming one, 2; two meanings of, 177–78

Zanta, Léonide, 151

Zen Buddhism, 115